THE FRAUD OF MONEY & BANKING

"THE BIRTH OF THE NEW FINANCIAL ORDER"

VOLUME THREE

A WRITTEN
DOCUMENTARY

"THE FRAUD OF THE FRAUD"

THE FRAUD OF MONEY & BANKING

"THE BIRTH OF THE NEW FINANCIAL ORDER"

VOLUME THREE
"DARUS TALED"

A WRITTEN DOCUMENTARY

Prepared & Translated by:

Jose M. Paulino

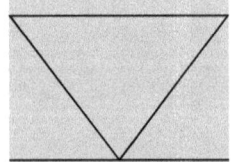

The Fraud of the Fraud: The Fraud of Money and Banking/
Volume Three

ISBN: 1440463476

EAN-13: 9781440463471

Printed in the United States of America

Research has been funded by OneSource Financial

COVER DESIGNED BY:
Jose M. Paulino

For more information, or to place an order for other books written by Jose M. Paulino, go to: http://factsmovement.com/

Contact Info:
Thefraud12@gmail.com

The Fraud of The Fraud

A Series of Written Documentaries Prepared and Translated by Jose M. Paulino

Volume One: The Conspiracy Theory Fraud
Volume Two: The War on Terror Fraud
Volume Three: The Fraud of Money & Banking
Volume Four: The Fraud of The Legal System
Volume Five: The Fraud of Religion

Publications

Publication # 1: The Good News
Publication #2: The Year 2012 AD, And What To Expect

"If the American people only understood the rank injustice of our money and banking system there would be a revolution before morning..."

-Andrew Jackson
7th U.S. President

About the Author

Jose Paulino is a former Wall Street Stockbroker with a degree in business. He has been researching and studying the power structure of the criminal elite for over 18 years. He is the author and creator of a new series of written documentaries entitled, *"THE FRAUD OF THE FRAUD."*

-DEDICATIONS-

I would like to dedicate this work to all who are a part of the struggle against the Unknowns and the criminal elite. I hope you enjoy the ideas and information presented in this written documentary. And while some of the ideas may be already familiar to you, I am certain that you will come across many which are not.

-Jpaul

Contents

INTRODUCTION

This documentary was written to expose the criminal elite who are in control of our monetary system. Most of us understand (to a certain degree) that the financial institutions are criminal. However, because the average person does not know how money is created or how the banking system works, they cannot put their finger on the deception. For instance, most people in the United States understand that the banker bailout bill that was passed in October of 2008, and the more recent bill passed by the Obama administration on February 17, 2009, are not equitable for the people. And yet, when speaking to the average person on the street, they cannot explain why the bill is corrupt.

The goal of this book is to teach you the basics of the financial structure in the United States. This book will take you from the birth of the banking concept, right up to today's current economic collapse. You will learn of what takes place with your money when you make a deposit in your bank. You will also learn what happens behind the scenes when you borrow money. There are many misconceptions that will also be addressed concerning depositors and borrowers. This documentary attempts to correct some of the false information that is commonly parroted within the truth movement. The misinformation is usually given by two types of people. There are those who mean well, and there are those who become front men for the agenda of the criminal elite. Those who mean well do not really understand money and banking. The most common misconceptions deal with fractional reserve banking and the Federal Reserve System. Banking misconceptions have caused good people to lose their homes, cars, and large sums of money.

This book attempts to cure some of those defects. A lie cannot survive in the presence of truth. When the truth comes, falsehoods must perish. A lie could only exist if the truth is absent. As we learn how money is created and how the banking system works, we will be better suited to expose their Ponzi schemes. They have purposely made financial language difficult to follow. This difficulty serves to make you disinterested in learning how the system really works. If you study and master this book, you will know what the economists know—minus the useless technical jargon. You will learn why the United States is in debt and how the economy is manipulated throughout its booms and busts. It will be made clear that the economic cycle is a total fraud. This fraud is the elementary cause of the innate volatility in our economy.

-JPaul

"So let me get this straight, you are going to lend me the money your customers have deposited?"
"Yes, but we will only take your property if you don't repay the money with interest. Is that fair enough?"

"The rich ruleth over the poor, And the borrower is servant to the lender."

-Proverbs 22:7

Volume Three

"THE FRAUD OF MONEY AND BANKING"

THE FRAUD OF MONEY AND BANKING

CHAPTER I.

THE BEGINNINGS OF BANKING

According to Blacks Law Dictionary, the definition of a bank is as follows:

> ***"A bank is an institution, usually incorporated, whose business it is to receive money on deposit, cash checks or drafts, discount commercial paper, make loans, and issue promissory notes payable to bearer, known as bank notes. U.C.C. 1-201(4). American commercial banks fall into two main categories: state chartered banks and federally chartered national banks." See also*** **Banking.**

Blacks Law Dictionary Abridged Sixth Edition *p.* 98.

The central meaning or definition of the word "bank" may vary from country to country. Nevertheless, the first modern day bank was founded in Italy *circa* 1406 at a city called Genoa. The name of the bank was *Banco di San Giorgio* (Bank of Saint George). To keep it simple, the very word "bank" comes from the Latin-Roman word *bancu*—the word for bench. This term was resurrected during the Renaissance Age by bankers who made their transactions above a bench. Going back to its root, the ancient Roman bankers had stalls that where referred to as *Macella,* meaning; on a long bench. The ancient Romans referred to this set up as a *bancu*. However, in those days bankers had a very limited roll. In most cases, they merely served as the institutions that converted foreign money into the Roman Imperial Mint.

Today's lending practices and the creation of paper money as applied by banks can be traced back to the goldsmiths of Medieval Europe. In those days many people stored their gold with the goldsmith. In return, the goldsmith would issue a receipt to the customer. The receipt would state the amount of gold the customer had in storage. This created demand deposits and bearer on demand notes.[1] This was also the beginning of the end for the bartering system that had been in place since the dawn of man. Instead of trading cows for pigs, or pigs for blankets, people began mostly trading cows, pigs, blankets, and services for their gold or silver receipts. This type of exchange created a longer storage time for gold and silver in the vaults of the goldsmiths.

Once the goldsmiths realized that only a small fraction of people were presenting these receipts to demand their gold at any one time, they found that they could write more receipts than the actual amount of gold they had in storage. This enabled the goldsmiths to loan out the extra receipts (money) and charge interest on those receipts. This was the birth of what is now known as "fractional reserved banking." It was a scam then and it is a scam today. The difference is that those who work behind the scenes have managed to get laws passed to make this

[1] A bearer on demand note is a bill or draft payable in lawful money upon presentation or demand.

scam legal. Today the scam takes place when you go to a bank and get a loan. They are lending you money that they do not own. Because the depositors will not withdraw their money at the same time, banks know they can lend that money and charge interest on it. Then, if you do not pay back your loan, they will take real tangible property. They will take your house, car, boat, and the shirt off your back!

Can you see this fraud? They are basically getting something for nothing. This is nothing more than a sophisticated system of deception. This is also how they control the money supply. All they really have to do is reduce the amount of receipts (money) in circulation. This would force the borrowers into insolvency, allowing the bank to then foreclose on property they bought with other peoples bank deposits, or non-existing receipts (money). It is this same system that has been implemented time and time again to snatch your property from under your feet. Throughout the entire world monetary systems have been put together in ways to primarily serve the needs of the wealthiest and most powerful residents on the planet.

With the implementation of credit cards and debit cards, less people are withdrawing their cash from banks. This is reminiscent of the goldsmiths and the demand receipts. Consumers are probably withdrawing about 1% of actual reserves.

> **41. What is the fractional reserve method of banking?**
>
> The fractional reserve method of banking originated with the goldsmiths—the predecessors of our present bankers. It is the method of banking in use today. Briefly, it is a system whereby bankers maintain as reserves only a fraction of the amount needed to meet

***Source*: Money Facts: *169 Questions and Answers on Money- a Supplement to A Primer on Money, with Index, Subcommittee on Domestic Finance.* United States Congress. House. Banking and Currency Committee, Published 1964, p.8**

Banking in the Ancient world

The key ingredients of banking may date back to the great civilizations of old. In ancient Babylon, commercial instruments were inscribed on clay tablets. The tablets usually stipulated for the payment of a certain weight of silver or gold. Today most of these tablets can still be seen in the British Museum. Many of these clay tablets contained records of deeds, partitions of real estate, bookkeeping entries, and loans of silver at interest. The oldest known laws concerning commercial transactions are found in the Code of Hammurabi. The Code of Hammurabi (*Codex Hammurabi*) is the best preserved ancient code of law. It dominated commercial transactions in ancient Babylon and most parts of the Middle East circa 1760 BC.

By the ninth century BC, the bankers had spread to Assyria. While in that country, the creation of commercial instruments evolved into what we now know as promissory notes, bills of exchange,[2] and transfer checks. This modern system was used without, or very little use of coined money. These financial contracts were inscribed on small clay tablets that were about the same size as a bar of soap. Naturally, these clay tablets could not be endorsed or accepted by signature, as is the case with our modern negotiable instruments. Instead, the presence of witnesses—usually someone who had religious or legal clout—would suffice for a legal endorsement of the commercial

[2] A bill of exchange is a kind of check or promissory note without interest. Bills of exchange developed during the Middle Ages as a means of transferring funds and making payments over long distances without physically moving bulky quantities of precious metals. In the hands of thirteenth century Italian merchants, bankers, and foreign exchange dealers, the bill of exchange evolved into a powerful financial tool, accommodating short-term credit transactions as well as facilitating foreign exchange transactions.

tablet. The Original was put inside the religious temples or government buildings. After the original was stored, copies were given to both parties.

From Assyria, the bankers spread to Greece. While in Greece, the bankers were subject to some regulation by the Greek governing body. The bankers of Athens were the most powerful in Greece. In those days banking was normally intermingled with foreign trade, and merchant services. The earliest forms of banking carried the responsibility of exchanging foreign monies for domestic monies and returning the foreign monies back to the country of origin. In Athens, negotiable instruments (written on clay tablets) were negotiated from the Middle East and Egypt. It was the Athenians who brought banking to the Romans. In fact, this knowledge of banking may have contributed to the rise of the Roman Empire. As Rome became a world power, the scope of Roman banking gradually extended to their conquered lands. This resulted in the creation of a complete body of jurisprudence known as, *The Institute of Justinian.*[3]

After Rome conquered all of Europe, the Europeans inherited the banking methods of their Roman masters. Although commerce and banking as practiced by the Romans barely survived the invasion of the barbarians, it persisted during the first part of the Middle-Ages. However, during this period the lack of security and the neglect of commerce created narrower limits on credit and banking. The rebirth of banking in the later Middle-Ages came

---

[3] The Justinian Code or *Corupus Iurus Civilis*, was the result of Emperor Justinian's aspiration that existing Roman law be collected into a simple and clear system of laws, or "code." Tribonian, a legal minister under Justinian, lead a group of scholars in a 14-month effort to codify existing Roman law. The result was the first Justinian Code, completed in 529 AD. This code was later expanded to include Justinian's own laws, as well as two additional books on areas of the law. In 534 AD, the Justinian Code, made up of the Code, the Digest, and the Institutes, was completed.

through the infamous money-changers.[4] As early as the eleventh century AD, the growth of commerce along with the accumulation of capital caused wealthy men to draw their precious metals from their hiding places and create their own coins for trade. The diversity of weights and the different market ratios between gold and silver made the function of the money-changers a very important. This caused the edicts of Leo the Wise, the Byzantine Emperor of Constantinople. The edicts created a series of provisions to govern the money-changers. Today, banking rules over religion. It is the main vehicle that controls the population. However, in the days of old, religion ruled above the bankers. In Europe, the Pope became the underlying authority on religion, government, law, and banking. However, the bankers were very useful to the church. They would transmit to the church contributions collected in other parts of the world. These bankers were given special protection as representatives of the pope. One such group of bankers were the Lombard's. originally from Northern Europe, the Lombard's were a Germanic people that settled in the valley of the Danube. They invaded the area of Byzantine, Italy in 568 AD under the leadership of King Alboin. It was the first established Anglo-Saxon Kingdom in Italy. Their reign lasted until 774 AD, when they were conquered by the Franks (a different Germanic tribe).

For centuries the Lombard bankers were rivaled by Jewish bankers. Neither one of these banking groups were popular with the people. The Lombard's shared with the Jews the unpopularity of their profession. As far away as France, their reputation as bankers was not a favorable one. This castration may have led to the mixing of the two groups. Several centuries later, many Lombard groups

---

[4] A money-changer was a person whose business entailed exchanging the money of one country for that of another country. In the bible, Jesus was angered by the money-changers and overturned their "macella" or benches (referred to in the King James Bible as "tables"). Refer to: Mark 11:15–19, 11:27–33, Matthew 21:12–17, 21:23–27, Luke 19:45–48, 20:1–8, and John 2:12–25.

were known to have been Jewish. In 1256, King Louis IX of France ordered 150 money-changers to be thrown in prison and the money they had loaned in France was confiscated. This act was similar to the arrest of the Knights Templar—which took place 51 years later. The Knights Templar are known to have been elite bankers. In fact the Knights Templar occupied and dominated the ranks of the goldsmiths in Europe during the Middle Ages. The war between the *Old World Order* and the *New World Order* is not new. This war has been going on for over a thousand years. Most historians agree that it was Pope Clement who gave the order to disband the Knights Templar.[5] Although there is no direct evidence to suggest that the church was directly involved with the arrest of the money-changers in 1256, King Louis IX was considered to be a religious king. He is known as "Saint Louis." In the United States, the city of St. Louis, which is located in the state of Missouri, is named after King Louis IX. Missouri was one of the states acquired from France through the Louisiana Purchase.[6] America kept the name in honor of the king, who was a

---

[5] It was King Philip IV of France who pressured Pope Clement V to take action against the Knights Templar. This was due in part because the French Crown was in deep debt to the Knights Templar.

[6] The Louisiana Purchase has been described as the "Greatest real estate deal in history." In 1803, The United States Government purchased the Louisiana Territory from Napoleon I of France for 60 million Francs, or, about $15,000,000. Originally, Napoleon had envisioned a great French empire in the New World. He hoped to use the Mississippi Valley as a food and trade center to supply the island of Hispaniola (Haiti/Dominican Republic), which was to be the heart of the French empire. First, however, he had to restore French control of Hispaniola, where Haitian slaves and kidnapped Africans, under TOUSSAINT L'OUVERTURE, had seized power in 1801. In 1802 a large army sent by Napoleon under his brother-in-law, Charles Leclerc, arrived on the island to suppress the Haitian rebellion. Despite some military success, the French lost thousands of soldiers, mainly to yellow fever, and Napoleon soon realized that Hispaniola must be abandoned. Without that island, he had little use for the Louisiana territory.

tertiary (3rd Degree) of the Order of the Holy Trinity (the Trinitarians). After King Louis IX's death in 1297, he was canonized into sainthood by Pope Boniface VIII. It is an accepted fact that the papacy turned sour on the money-changers. This led to the showdown with the most significant money-changers of them all—The Knights Templar.

It is said that a noble Frenchman by the name of Hugues de Payens (the first Grand-Master of the Templars) gathered-up eight of his knight relatives in the year 1119 AD and formed the order. Some people are in denial of the fact that the Knights Templar survived the October 13th surprise attacks and integrated (as well as formed) with other secret societies. The Freemasonic orders of the Rose and the Cross (Rosicrucian's) are directly linked to the Knights Templar. By the middle of the twelfth century AD, the Templars mission of making sure that Christian pilgrims reached the holy land safely took a dramatic turn. Instead of guarding the pilgrims, the Knights Templar began to guard the pilgrim's valuables. To avoid being robbed on the way to the holy land, pilgrims would visit a Templar building in their home country and deposit their deeds and valuables. The Templars would then issue them a note describing their valuables. Naturally the note holder could redeem the valuables upon presentment of the note. This was similar to what was taking place during the Middle Ages with the goldsmiths (also Templars).

[7]

[7] This Templar Seal is said to have been showing Hugues de Payens and Godfrey de Saint-Omer on one horse. Although the Templars were forbidden to share horses, one of the main line interpretations of this symbol is said to represent the initial poverty of the order; they could afford only a single horse for every two men.

The History of Central Banking

A central bank is most commonly described as an authoritative bank responsible for setting policies. These policies affect a country's money supply and credit system. The Common functions of central banks the world over are open market operations, discount lending (to commercial banks only), and setting reserve requirements.

The earliest forms of central banking dates back to at least the seventeenth century AD in the form of what is known as the *Swedish Riksbank*. In 1668, the bank was established as a joint-stock bank authorized to lend the government money and act as a clearing house for commercial purposes.

The world's oldest note-issuing institution was the antecedent of the Swedish Riksbank. The antecedent bank was known as *Stockholms Banco* or the Bank of Palmstruch. It was named after its founder in 1656, Johan Palmstruch. The bank eventually collapsed as a result of issuing too many bank notes without the necessary collateral to repay depositors. This collapse caused the prohibition of the Riksbank to issue bank notes. However, in 1701, permission to issue bank notes was once again granted to the Riksbank. The catch, however, was that the bank had to regard the notes as "credit-notes." A credit note is a note issued to a person or corporation when merchandise is returned. Nevertheless, these credit-notes caused a major problem. The problem was caused by the counterfeit notes that began to appear in circulation. In order to prevent this counterfeiting, the Riksbank created its very own special paper for the credit-notes. In 1755 the bank founded the Tumba Bruk printing company and began to manufacture the new Swedish Krona bank-notes. By the nineteenth century AD, the Riksbank had a dominant role as the top credit institution and issuer of bank notes. For the most part, early central banks issued private notes that served as currency. These banks often had a monopoly over issuing private notes.

The big kahuna of central banks is the Bank of England. The Bank of England was nationalized[8] in March of 1946 and gained independence in 1997. This English bank was founded by Sir William Paterson[9] and was granted a royal charter with the passage of the *Tonnage Act* of 1694. Hardly coincidental, this bank was originally built on the same exact location that housed the ancient temple of the god Mithras.[10] The worship of Mithras was brought to London by its Roman founders circa 47 AD.

***Refer* to: http://www.bankofengland.co.uk/about/index.htm**

The Bank of England is indeed the house that Rothschild's built. The first and second central banks in America were patterned after the Bank of England. Some argue as to where the seat of power resides for the elite bankers (New York or London). In my estimation, it is a moot point. The simple fact is that the criminal elite control both sides of the Atlantic.

---

[8] Nationalization occurs when an industry or certain assets are taken to be owned by the public of a national government. It is historically a more recent development than and differs in motive and degree from "expropriation" or "eminent domain," which is the right of government to take property for particular public purposes.

[9] Sir William Paterson was also influential in the establishment of the Bank of Scotland (1695), the central bank of the Kingdom of Scotland. Sir William Paterson is to not be mistaken with the New Jersey States-man and signor of the United States Constitution, William Paterson, who was born December 24, 1745 and died on September 9, 1806).

[10] The Romans first encountered the cult of Mithras in Persia (modern Iran) during the reign of the Emperor Nero. However, the origins of Mithras in India have been traced back to 1400 BC. One of the many mystery cults that the Romans introduced from the east, Mithraism first appealed to slaves and freedmen, but the cult's emphasis on truth, honor, courage, and its demand for discipline soon led to Mithras becoming a god of soldiers, traders, merchants, and bankers.

First Bank of the United States

The First Bank of the United States (1791-1811) was granted a twenty-year charter by Congress in 1791. This bank was not the first actual bank in the country. It was, however, the first central bank established in the new republic called America.

The bill to authorize the bank was introduced into Congress on December 13, 1790. It passed the Senate on January 20, 1791, the House on February 8, 1791, and was forwarded to President Washington for his signature. At first, George Washington was skeptical of signing the bill. James Madison, Thomas Jefferson, and the Attorney General Edmund Randolph argued that the Constitution had not granted the government the power to incorporate a central bank. However, other prominent figures of that time were also in George Washington's ear promoting the bank. Those in favor of the bank made a compelling argument. Proponents of the bank (such as Alexander Hamilton) argued that the bank was necessary because the country was in debt as a result of the Revolutionary War. During this time, each state issued their own money. The new central bank would create a standard form of money that would be accepted throughout the nation.

Alexander Hamilton, who was the Secretary of the Treasury under George Washington, spear headed the creation of the bank. Alexander Hamilton was one of many minions that the British bankers had installed in America. Most historians agree that Hamilton admired England's political and financial construct. Hamilton preached and petitioned for a broader central government and more implied powers for the federal government.

All-in-all, Hamilton's bank was mostly supported by the Northern States. This was perhaps due to the merchant nature of the economy in the north. The Southern States, whose chief industry was agriculture, did not require centrally concentrated banks. They viewed the bank in a different light. Their views against the bank had more to do with states' rights. Southerners were content with their own local banks. During this era, the Southern States had their suspicions of the Northern states. Of course, those suspicions led all the way up to the Civil War.

Meanwhile, Alexander Hamilton was the chief negotiator of the first loan obtained by the U.S. Government in 1789. The amount of $200,000 was issued by the Bank of New York. It was founded by Hamilton and a banker by the name of Aaron Burr. Originally the name of the bank was to be called *The First Bank of Manhattan*. This was the first bank created in the city of New York (Wall St). The Bank, of course, was financed by the Bank of England. Hamilton and Burr secured a charter from the Bank of England for a private company that was to be used to improve the water supply of Manhattan. The surplus capital from the water supply venture was then used to establish the Bank of New York. Out of 25,000 shares, 18,000 were held by investors in England. The Bank of England now had their paws on the American financial scene. Eventually, the Bank of England became the chief creditor of the United States.

How was the United States going to pay the interest on the loans? During this era, there was no personal income tax (as it was deemed unconstitutional). Consequently, Alexander Hamilton proposed an excise tax on alcohol. This imposed tax led to the Whiskey Rebellion.[11]

---

[11] Angered by an excise tax imposed on whiskey in 1791 by the federal government, farmers in the western counties of Pennsylvania engaged in a series of violent attacks on excise tax agents. The tax effectively eliminated any profit by the farmers from the sale or barter of an important cash crop, and became the lightning rod for a wide variety of grievances by the settlers of the region against the federal government. The rebellion was short lived after President Washington sent in the Militia.

Second Bank of the United States

After the First Bank of the United States' charter expired in 1811, there was much debate as to whether it should be renewed. However, President James Madison did not renew the banks charter. This did not sit well with the banking cartels. The British set out to disrupt the American economy by imposing a series of trade restrictions that the United States contested as illegal under international law. This riff caused the United States to declare war on Britain and thus begin the War of 1812. Unfortunately, the war made matters worse by adding an extra burden on the American economy. This burden caused President Madison to give into the banker's request. In an attempt to stabilize the economy, Madison's administration granted the Second Bank of the United States a charter in 1816. But the bank was challenged by the state of Maryland in the land mark case of *McCulloch v. Maryland* 17 U.S. 316 (1819). The U.S. Supreme Court upheld the central banks legality under the authority of the *Necessary-and-Proper Clause* found in Article I of the United States Constitution, section viii, clause 18:

> ***"The Congress shall have Power - To make all Laws which shall be necessary and proper for carrying into Execution the foregoing Powers, and all other Powers vested by this Constitution in the Government of the United States, or in any Department or Officer thereof."***

This basically means that any state law contrary to a federal law is null and void (as long as the federal law is constitutional). Notwithstanding, the bank still faced resistance and criticism from the public and government officials alike. The bank was considered the main cause of the panic and economic recession of 1819. The banks official position was that it could not have prevented the economic downturn due to the fact that $4 million was due to the European investors who bought bonds from the United States in order to fund the *Louisiana Purchase.*[12] The bank was required to make this payment as the government's fiscal agent. This caused the bank to call the loans it had lent commercial banks. This caused a severe tightening of the money supply.

Perhaps the biggest problem was that the European investors were to be paid in gold or silver. The loans made to most commercial banks at the time had been made in the form of fiat paper. The bank then forced commercial banks to repay the fiat loans in gold or silver. This made the money supply run low even after several years of inflated currency and rampant speculation based on debt. To put it in simpler terms, the real money (gold and silver) was being shipped to Europe, and the fiat (non-redeemable paper) was to become the medium of exchange in America. All of this caused the Second Bank to fall out of favor with too many people. On July 10, 1832, President Andrew Jackson put a veto on the banks request to be rechartered. In President Jackson's veto message, he states the following:

> *"Is there no danger to our liberty and independence in a bank that in its nature has so little to bind it to our country? The president of the bank has told us that most of the State banks exist by its forbearance. Should its influence become concentered, as it may under the operation of such an act as this, in the hands of a self-elected directory whose interests are identified with those of the foreign stockholders, will there not be cause to tremble for the purity of our elections in peace and for the independence of our country in war? Their power would be great whenever they might choose to exert it; but if this monopoly*

---

[12] The Louisiana Purchase was territory bought from France in 1803. The territory is measured at about 828,800 square miles. The Louisiana Purchase encompassed portions of 15 current U.S. states and 2 Canadian Provinces.

were regularly renewed every fifteen or twenty years on terms proposed by themselves, they might seldom in peace put forth their strength to influence elections or control the affairs of the nation. But if any private citizen or public functionary should interpose to curtail its powers or prevent a renewal of its privileges, it can not be doubted that he would be made to feel its influence."[13]

President Jackson exercised his authority to issue this veto and inform the American people of the dangers such a bank can pose to their liberty. One of the biggest concerns that President Jackson had was the foreign ownership of the bank. He referred to the bank as a "Monopoly" held by foreigners and "A few hundred of our own citizens—chiefly—of the richest class."

The president's veto passed and the bank was defeated (for the moment). The bank continued to serve as the depository institution for Federal Funds until 1833, at which time President Jackson ordered the Secretaries of the Treasury to remove existing deposits and discontinue using the Bank for future deposits of federal funds. Nevertheless, the heads of the U.S. Treasury Department, Louis McLane and William John Duane, refused to follow President Jackson's order. This led to their removal and the appointment of Roger B. Taney, who was President Jackson's former attorney general and an opponent of the bank. After the banks twenty year federal charter expired in 1836, it attempted to function as a regular bank. However, it fell and ceased its operations by 1841. Unfortunately, the bankers were relentless and continued their quest to gain control of the U.S. monetary system. This is the main ingredient the bankers needed to take over the country. They realized it did not matter if foreigners owned the stock. The important thing was controlling the monetary policy. Therefore, in order to sneak the bank passed the

[13] Read the complete veto message in the back of this book at Appendix- A

American people, they seceded to many of the arguments that made the people nervous. They tweaked a couple of things and gave us THE FEDERAL RESERVE SYSTEM. The key points of the Federal Reserve Act are: (1) Foreigners cannot own stock; (2) The seven members of the Board of Governors are nominated by the President of the United States and confirmed by the U.S. Senate. (3) And lastly, the bank is not for profit. After the passing of the Federal Reserve Act, the bankers were back in the catbird seat. All they needed was a deep recession or depression, after which, the total takeover of the monetary system and monopoly on issuing money would become exclusively theirs.

Before the passing of the Federal Reserve Act of 1913, the U.S. economy had a rather steady growth. This was a result of matching the money in circulation with the goods and services in the economy. However, after 1913, the country's economy began having large booms and large busts. Money faded from gold and silver notes, gold and silver certificates, to non-redeemable legal tender. It is very important to know that the paper money that we have today is not backed by gold or silver. It is only backed by your labor (slavery). If you take a look at the upper left hand side of the U.S. dollar bill, you will see it in plain site. You will see that you are holding a note. It is not the same exact thing as having your car note in your pocket, but the concept is similar. A note is simply an IOU. A payer has promised to pay someone else, called a beneficiary, some money. However, since a Federal Reserve note is already legal tender (money), what is promised on the note? It seems complicated, since Federal Reserve notes are not redeemable in gold, silver or any other commodity, and they receive no backing by anything of material value. This process was started in 1933. Today, the notes have no value on their own except for what they will buy. In other words, because they are legal tender, Federal Reserve notes are theoretically backed by all the goods and services in the U.S. economy.

Refer to: http://www.ustreas.gov/education/faq/currency/legal-tender.shtml

Once upon a time, U.S. currency was backed by gold or silver. Notice the difference on this $5 dollar bill below. The Text in the box reads; "REDEEMABLE IN GOLD ON DEMAND AT THE UNITED STATES TREASURY OR IN GOLD OR LAWFUL MONEY AT ANY FEDERAL RESERVE BANK."

These Federal Reserve notes were the obligation of the Federal Reserve. They are not the same currency as United States notes. United States notes were authorized by the *Legal Tender Act* of 1862. United States notes are obligations of the United States Government the same as any government issued bonds or issued treasury bills. Because the current Federal Reserve notes were not issued to raise revenue in the like manner of treasury bills and government bonds, the Federal Reserve now had a monopoly on issuing United States currency. Tragically, United States notes were eventually discontinued on January 21, 1971.

This note is legal tender
for one dollar.

This dollar shown above was issued by the United States Government in 1917. This dollar is not a Federal Reserve note. The top arrow above points to the following; "THIS NOTE IS LEGAL TENDER FOR ONE DOLLAR." It basically means that what is owed on this note is one dollar. Today's dollar bill reads something different. It is legal tender "for all debts." This means the dollar you have in your pocket is backed by debt (labor) and is accepted for value. To put it simply, they are worth what people believe they are worth. However, contrary to popular belief by those of us involved in the Truth Movement, the Federal Reserve's charter does provide for Federal Reserve notes to be exchanged for gold or silver coins at any Federal Reserve Bank. This clause is purposely kept absent from today's Federal Reserve notes. Why is the redemption clause kept absent from today's Federal Reserve notes? The old Federal Reserve notes had the following language written on the face of the bill:

"Will pay to the bearer on demand"
"Redeemable in gold or lawful money at any Federal Reserve Bank."

The recognition of what a note entails no longer appears on the face of Federal Reserve notes. There is no longer a statement to clarify whether the note can be redeemed. Notice that the Federal Reserve note does not bother to point out that the note is "lawful money." The note simply states: *"This Note Is Legal Tender For All Debts Public And Private."*

Below is a copy of the first Federal Reserve note issued in 1914. At the time this was issued, a note was well understood to be a promise of payment. Accordingly, this is prominently labeled as a Federal Reserve Bank Note.

And what is this note redeemable in? Here is what it reads: *"Secured By United States Certificates Of Indebtedness Or One-Year Gold Notes, Deposited With The Treasurer Of The United States Of America."* The note was directly redeemable in U.S. Treasury debt, but it was not directly redeemable in gold.

Today's Federal Reserve notes are fiat in nature. Many believe this is the main reason why the money supply is easily manipulated. However, currency backed by gold and silver can also be manipulated. All the banks have to do is buy up gold and silver while reducing the amount of notes in circulation that are redeemable (in gold or silver). This would cause the money supply to dry up, leaving businesses with insufficient money to pay employees and pay for expenses.

Another negative of having a currency backed by gold or silver would occur if all the currency in circulation was redeemed. What would the currency be backed with if that took place? As an example, the panic of 1837 was caused, in part, because the Bank of England (an ally of the Second Bank of the U.S.) restricted the flow of gold and silver coins (specie) to the United States. This caused a shortage of gold and silver that led to a fall in cotton prices and collateral in most American loans, which required specie.[14] These loans became harder to acquire, cotton became devalued, and the U.S. economy suffered.

I will continue stressing this because we need to understand; it makes no difference whether we have a fiat currency,[15] or a currency backed by commodities—such as gold or silver. There only needs to be enough money in circulation to satisfy the demand for it. In other words, money should only serve the economy to facilitate trade.

---

[14] The word specie comes from the Latin. It means "in kind" or "in the same or like form". Specie refers to paper money that was considered to be the same or like having coins, either gold or silver. Most dictionaries define specie as gold or silver coins.

[15] A *fiat money* is an object used as a medium of exchange that will never be used as a consumption good or a productive input. More precisely, Wallace (1980) defines *fiat money* to be money that is intrinsically useless and inconvertible. Intrinsic uselessness refers to the property that the object will never be used as a consumption good nor as a production good, while *inconvertibility* refers to the fact that it is not backed by something that has intrinsic worth.
***Source*: Federal Reserve Bank of Minneapolis Quarterly Review Summer 1992, Volume 16, No. 3- page 2**

THE FRAUD OF MONEY AND BANKING

CHAPTER II.

FRACTIONAL RESERVE BANKING

Fractional Reserved banking is basically defined as;

> ***The portion (expressed as a percent) of depositors' balances banks must have on hand as cash. This is a requirement determined by the country's central bank, which in the U.S. is the Federal Reserve. The reserve ratio affects the money supply in a country.***

***Sources*: *The Bank Credit Analysis Handbook: A Guide for Analysts, Bankers and Investors* by Jonathan Golin. Also refer to; http://www.bankintroductions.com/definition.html**

Since its beginnings, banking has always been an integral part of any successful economic system. Unfortunately, banking has evolved into a criminal ingredient used to enslave the people.

Early bankers, such as the Lombard's and the Jewish bankers of Europe, were merchants first and bankers second. They loaned money from the excess profits of their mercantile activities and extended credit to their customers. And in the case of these great banking families, the banking part of their operations eventually overtook the merchant part of their daily business activities. These bankers loaned money out of their own profits and earned interest from those loans. Eventually, the banking profession began to add certain practices that became detrimental to the people and their economy. One of the more noticeable practices is considered to be fractional reserve banking.

Many of us in the truth movement are under the supposition that fractional reserve banking is a fraud committed against depositing customers. In order to understand how the banking elite have made themselves immune from lawfully committing fraud, we need to understand that your deposit is defined as "a loan" to the bank. According to Black's Law Dictionary, the Eighth Edition published by Thomson West (2004), a loan is defined as:

> **loan**, *n.* **1**. An act of lending; a grant of something for temporary use. **2**. A thing lent for the borrower's temporary use; esp., a sum of money lent at interest.
>
> *p.* 954

As a matter of law, the bank is covered of any wrong doing by paying the depositor interest on the deposit. This basically means that when you deposit money in a bank, it is to be (in actuality) defined as "a loan" to the bank. Therefore, according to law, the bank may lend or invest the bulk of your deposit in accordance with the fractional reserve requirement set by the fed.

If we are going to win this war, we need to understand these types of tricks. The government, the bankers, and the lawmakers[16] are all working together against the people.

---

[16] The lawmakers in this case also include judges and lawyers; not just the legislature.

Fractional Reserve Banking; An Example

Fractional Reserve banking is the facet that allows banks to create money. Fractional reserve banking is also what has many people making the claim that banks create money "out of thin air." Do banks create money out of thin air? You can make that claim only with the understanding that the money is created by the borrowers and depositors. Such a claim can confuse people into believing that banks can print money at their whim and lend it out to the public. How does it all work? Let us make this simple so that a sixth grader would understand it. Without question, there is a terrible amount of mis-info that has been infused into the truth movement concerning how fractional reserve banking works.

How it works; let us say Frank opens a bank account and deposits $100 dollars into that account paying him 3% interest. Let us also say the banks reserve requirement is 10% as set by the Federal Reserve.[17] This means that the bank must keep $10 out of that $100 it deposited in its vault. Banks must meet the reserve requirement by law. Are we clear on that? As far as Frank is concerned, he has a bank account worth $100. As far as the bank is concerned, it has a $100 deposit of which it may loan out $90. This is all a result of the banks right to only keep 10% of any money deposited.

The math looks like this; $100 X .1(10%) = $10. Now enters the next costumer to ask for a loan. Let us call him Tony. The bank informs Tony that it could loan him up to $90 charging 6% interest. Tony accepts the terms and the loan is made. Frank still has $100 in his account, but now Tony has $90 as well. The $90 dollars can be said to have been created out of thin air. However, a more accu-

---

[17] According to the Monetary Control Act of 1980, they must hold between 8 and 14 percent of their checking (not total) deposits in reserve, as specified by the fed.

rate term would be “money expansion.” Franks $100 deposit has been expanded to $190. But wait, there is more. The bank now has a negotiable instrument called a note. The note is the loan (contract) that Tony created by putting his signature on a piece of paper promising to pay the bank money that, although really belongs to Frank, is on the face of the note as belonging to the bank. The bank can now take this note and either sell it for value, or borrow money from the Federal Reserve Bank at a steep discounted rate of interest. Let us say the bank sold the note to another bank for $75. The bank can now start this whole process again as it is only required to hold $7.50 out of the $75.

The bank that bought the note for only $75 can now go to the Federal Reserve Bank and use the $90 note (that was created by Tony) as collateral to borrow $90 at a discounted rate. The $90 that they receive from the Federal Reserve is deposited in their vault. But since they are only required to keep $9 out of that $90 in the vault, $81 can be loaned out to a customer and this whole process can start again. Remember, it started with only $100 of real money deposited by Frank. As the process continues, the banking system will expand Frank’s initial deposit of $100 into a maximum of $1,000 of money. The $75 for the sold note will expand to $750. That is a general outline of how fractional banking works.

Keeping with the same example, the path to the math would look like this:

($100+$90+81+$72.90+...=$1,000)
($75+$67.5+$60.75+$54.67+...=$750)

Although no new money was physically created in addition to Franks initial $100 deposit, new commercial bank money was created when his deposit was loaned out. When the reserve rate is 10%, as in Frank’s example, the maximum amount of total deposits that can be created is $1,000 and the maximum amount of commercial bank money that can be created is $900. For the bank, the deposit is considered a liability, whereas, the customer deposits that have been lent to others, and the reserves from those deposits, are considered assets. The deposit will always be equal to the loan plus the reserve—since the loan and reserve are created from the deposit.

The creation and retirement of most promissory notes (M3) occur through this process. Whether it is created or retired all depends on what direction the process moves. When the bank lends out its customers deposits, the process moves from the top down and money is created. When loans are paid back, the process moves from the bottom to the top and commercial bank money is retired and no longer negotiable. Negotiable instruments[18] dominate the money supply in any economy of the world. Such an instrument (M3) is valuable to banks because it can be sold to another bank for cash-money. In the United States, that cash would be Federal Reserve notes (M1).

This type of money expansion is measured by the money multiplier Formula.

According to businessdictionary.com, the money multiplier is defined as:

> **Mathematical relationship between the monetary base and money supply of an economy. It explains the increase in the amount of cash in circulation generated by the banks' ability to lend money out of their depositors' funds. When a bank makes a loan, it 'creates' money because the loan becomes a new deposit from which the borrower can withdraw cash to spend. This money-creating power is based on the fractional reserve system under which banks are required to keep at hand only a portion (between 10 to 15 percent, typically 12 percent) of the depositors'**

---

[18] By definition, cash is also a negotiable instrument. However, Federal Reserve notes (cash) are not negotiable via endorsement. Therefore, when referring to a negotiable instrument, cash is rarely ever implied.

funds. The rest may be converted into loans, thereby increasing the available cash by a factor that is a multiple of the initial deposit.

Refer to: http://www.businessdictionary.com/definition/money-multiplier.html

The money multiplier, *m*, is the inverse of the reserve requirement, *R*:

$$m = \frac{1}{R}$$

For example, with the reserve ratio of 10 percent, this reserve ratio, *R*, can also be expressed as a fraction:

$$R = \frac{1}{10}$$

So then the money multiplier, *m*, will be calculated as:

$$M = \frac{1}{1/10} = 10$$

This number is multiplied by the initial deposit to show the maximum amount of money it can be expanded to. All the while, this system is manipulated by the tightening and loosening of the money supply. The Federal Open Market Committee (FOMC) is charged with performing this task. The FOMC consists of twelve members. The members consist of the seven members of the Board of Governors of the Federal Reserve System, the president of the Federal Reserve Bank of New York, and four of the remaining eleven Federal Reserve Bank presidents—who serve one-year terms on a rotating basis.

The Federal Reserve act of 1913 gave the Federal Reserve the responsibility of setting monetary policy. This is how they are able to create and control the economic booms and busts.

***Sources*:**
http://www.newyorkfed.org/research/epr/02v08n1/0205benn/0205benn.html
http://www.federalreserve.gov/monetarypolicy/fomc.htm

In business school, students are taught about the economic cycle and how it is merely a fact of life. They are taught that no one can predict the booms or the busts due to the many variables that come into play. We must realize what they are doing. They purposely make things complicated in order to keep the people disinterested in learning the great game. Meanwhile, they do their simple devilishment behind all the smoke and mirror they create. Restricting fractional banking is vital if we want to have more control over the amount of money in circulation.

Fractional reserve banking is one of the primary reasons for our mounting private debt. This is adding considerably to the economic uncertainties that businesses and individuals are finding themselves at the mercy of. I do not discount the unethical practices of predatory lending. However, the mounting debt that plagues most people can be traced back to the abuses of fractional reserved banking. This is one of the key ingredients in the booms and busts of the economic cycle. It is all manipulated by the loosening and tightening of the money supply.

The fact that fractional reserve banking allows the banking system to create money is openly admitted by the Federal Reserve.

"The fact that banks are required to keep on hand only a fraction of the funds deposited with them is a function of the banking business. Banks borrow funds from their depositors (those with savings) and in turn lend those funds to the banks' borrowers (those in need of funds). Banks make money by charging borrowers more for a loan (a higher percentage interest rate) than is paid to depositors for use of their money. If banks did not lend out their available funds after meeting their reserve requirements, depositors might have to pay banks to provide safekeeping services for their money. For the economy and the banking system as a whole, the practice of keeping only a fraction of deposits on hand has an important cumulative effect. Referred to as the fractional reserve system, it permits the banking system to "create" money.

***Source*: Page 57 of 'The FED today', a publication released by the united states federal reserve education website designed to educate people on the history and purpose of the united states federal reserve system. http://www.federalreserveeducation.org/fed101/fedtoday/FedTodayAll.pdf**

Sympathizers of fractional reserve banking make an appealing case for its use. The argument for fractional reserve banking states that it allows the banks to loan out more money, hence, stimulating economic growth. I agree that without fractional reserve banking, the banks will have no money to lend. However, when you couple fractional reserve banking with the erratic loosening and tightening of the money supply, economic disasters are sure to follow. It becomes a matter of slow steady economic growth versus large booms and even larger busts. In reality, as long as the money in circulation is enough to satisfy the needs of the consumers according to the goods and services available in society, it would not matter whether there was fractional reserve banking. The problem is that banks abuse fractional reserve banking and engage in predatory lending tactics. Such tactics have ruined many financial lives forever. Meanwhile, when the consumer defaults, the bank receives a real tangible asset, i.e., houses, cars, yachts, etc. The bank then auctions or sells these assets at market value. The proceeds from those sales allow more money for the banks to either invest or re-lend.

I am not suggesting that you are not responsible for paying back borrowed money. I am suggesting that the terms of the "note" are never equitable for the borrower. Why do I say this? Because the bank never has anything at risk by lending you money that; 1) is not theirs, 2) is money that they themselves have borrowed from depositors. 3) The depositors will not demand all their deposits at any one time. 4) Usually, the bank no longer posses the note. Therefore, the bank is unjustly enriched[19] by getting something for nothing.

In the end, the loser of the deal is the borrower. The borrower loses the down payment (which the bank will re-lend and/or invest) and the property acquired.

---

[19] Unjust enrichment is a legal term denoting a particular type of causative event in which one party is unjustly enriched at the expense of another.

Money Expansion

Fractional reserve banking is the main cause of money expansion. Again, this expansion of money (as some say out of thin air) is caused by borrowing and depositing. This new type of money is what makes up the components of M1 and M3[20] statistics. In short, there are two types of money in a fractional reserve banking system. The borrower gets M1 (physical dollars or checking account) in exchange for M3 (The note/contract signed by borrowers). The bank can benefit in three ways from this transaction. The first is by collecting interest on the money (M1) it loaned the borrower in exchange for the note/contract. Keep in mind, this money does not really belong to the bank. It belongs to the banks depositing customers. Secondly, the bank may benefit by selling the note/contract (also known as a negotiable instrument) for a profit. Thirdly, it can present the note/contract as collateral to the Federal Reserve in exchange for Federal Reserve notes (money). This is usually done when the bank has no excess reserves to loan.[21] Usually, the loan from the fed is made for 15 days interest free. The bank then sells your note/contract into the secondary market. This is called rediscounting the debt. Banks may rediscount short-term debt securities to assist the movement of a market that has a high demand for loans. When there is low liquidity in the market, banks can generate cash by rediscounting short-term securities. This enables the bank the liquidity to cash the check that you have written from the loan you have obtained.

***Refer to*: http://www.frbdiscountwindow.org/mechanics.cfm?hdrID=14**

---

[20] In 2006, the Federal Reserve abolished publishing data on the M3 money supply.

[21] This happens when the bank cannot meet its reserve requirement as set by the Federal Reserve.

To sum up, the bank exchanges the note/contract (M3) for cash-money (M1). In theory, when the bank hypothecates[22] it's M3 (the loan/repurchase agreement),[23] the bank no longer has anything at risk in a contract with the borrower. The biggest scam occurs when a mortgage is rediscounted without notice to the mortgagor. Assigning the debt to the Federal Reserve has become common practice for commercial banks. This allows the lending institutions to borrow from the Federal Reserve at low interest rates. The scam is complete when the lenders introduce a copy of the note/contract as sufficient evidence to perfect a security interest to foreclose on your property. I know that may sound a bit confusing so let me elaborate. You exchanged M1 for M3 with the bank. When you repay (or give back) the banks M1, you are entitled to get the M3 (signed contract/note). At this point, the M3 (note/contract) is retired and not negotiable (not worth anything). The note/contract should be stamped paid or something to truly show that it has been settled.

Most people who are in default of their contracts are defrauded by the courts and the banks. The fraud occurs when the bank or the note holder does not present the original note as evidence of the debt. Think of it this way. It would be the same as if you presented copies of paper money to the court as evidence that you paid or intend to pay the M1 (money) you owe the bank. Do you see? If you cannot do that, why can they? They cannot! The following is from a New York Supreme Court foreclosure case. In this case, a mortgage company bought the

---

[22] To pledge something (of value) as security or collateral for a debt, without delivery of title or possession.

[23] Repurchase agreements (RPs or Repos) are financial instruments used in the money markets and capital markets. For instance, the holder of your car note can sell that note for cash if they promise to repurchase the note from the buyer (known as the cash provider) for a greater amount of money at some later date. That greater sum of money paid equals all of the cash lent and some extra cash (constituting the implicit interest rate, known as the *repo rate*).

mort-gage note from the original lenders. However, as in most cases, the original note was not given to the assignee (purchaser of the note).

The following case excerpt can be found at: Lasalle Bank National Association v. Lamy, 12 Misc.3d 1191(A), 824 N.Y.S.2d 769 (N.Y.Sup. 08/07/2006)

The opinion of the court was delivered by the Honorable Edward D. Burke, J.

Published by New York State Law Reporting Bureau pursuant to Judiciary Law § 431

"As this court indicated in its prior order of March 31, 2006, only the owner of the note and mortgage at the time of the commencement of a foreclosure action may properly prosecute said action (Kluge v Fugazy 145 AD2d 537, 536 NYS2d 92; see also, Katz v Eastville Realty Co., 249 AD2d 243, 672 NYS2d 308). To state a cognizable claim sounding in foreclosure, the complaint must contain, inter alia, allegations regarding the plaintiff's ownership interest in the note and mortgage which is the subject of the proceeding. Because ownership of both the note and mortgage at the time of the commencement of a mortgage foreclosure action is a necessary element of the plaintiff's cause of action for foreclosure of the mortgage, entry of a default judgment against the defendant mortgagors and others joined as party defendants is precluded where the plaintiff's ownership interest in both the note and the mortgage is not ascertainable from the pleadings and the documentation submitted in support of the motion (CPLR 3215; RPAPL 1321; see also Beaton v Transit Facility Corp, 14 AD3d 637, 789 NYS2d 314, and the cases cited therein; see also, Morgan v Bagayoko, 1 AD3d 582, 767 NYS2d 631).

It is axiomatic that to be effective, an assignment of a note and a mortgage given as security therefor must be made by the owner of such note and mortgage and that an assignments made by entities having no ownership interest in the note and mortgage pass no title therein to the assignee (see, (Matter of Stralem. 303 AD2d 120, 758 NYS2d 345, and the cases cited therein).

If they cannot produce the M3 (mortgage note), then they are not entitled to take your money and property. No contract is enforceable, of course, without the flow of consideration—both sides must get something out of the ex-change. See *Friedman v. Tappan Development Corp.*, 22 N.J. 523, 533 (1956); 1 A. Corbin, Contracts § 110 (1963 ed.). They cannot take your M1 without giving you back your M3!

The following article is not from a major financial authority. However, I could find no flaw in it. If anyone can find anything that is incorrect, I am all ears.

Make Sure the Bank Owns Your Loan if it is Suing for Foreclosure

June 26, 2008, 9:19 am
Posted by Admin in Legal Information
Rating: 0/5 Votes : 0

One of the more creative defenses to a foreclosure lawsuit that has surfaced in the past year is that of requesting the foreclosing bank to prove that it owns the mortgage note and has standing to sue the homeowners. In the vast majority of foreclosure actions, banks do not produce the original note, instead relying on the ignorance of homeowners not to challenge the bank's positions. But with the predatory lending and investing that went on during the boom years of the subprime mortgage industry, many of these loans have been sliced up and sold off piece by piece, packaged into mortgage-backed securities and sold to hedge funds, pension funds, and other investors. In fact, the originating mortgage companies may now be completely out of business, with the collapse of the subprime industry claiming over 250 lenders so far.

So the loans were originated by a company that is now out of business, and then it was sliced up and the rights to various parts of the mortgage were sold to other companies. But in order to sue for foreclosure, the bank initiating the lawsuit must have been assigned the mortgage, and investors in the mortgage-backed securities are not even assigned ownership in a specific property unless and until the homeowners fall behind on the payments. They have simply been bundled up into one huge pool of mortgages with no specific owners of any particular note. Thus, the companies that invested in these mortgage securities were not parties to the original transaction -- they never participated directly in the origination of the mortgage nor its subsequent sale. Investors are merely assigned to particular mortgages after the fact, and there was no true sale of the security to the investors, which is an element of a valid securities sale. Investors and banks, it seems, can not prove they own the mortgages, can not prove that they were assigned a particular mortgage that they are now suffering damage from its default, and can not show that they even bought a legitimate security.

And these are the companies that are presuming to sue homeowners for foreclosure! After doing everything they could to induce people into fraudulent loans and limit their own exposure to the inevitable defaults, banks are discovering that all of these shenanigans have only insulated them against actual ownership of the loan. So, because lenders <u>rely on the ignorance of homeowners</u> to foreclose anyway, this is the defense they have turned to for the majority of foreclosure cases. Many lenders are now submitting an affidavit to the courts that they <u>do not own the original loan</u> but they swear they have standing to complain against the homeowners. Essentially, they are just requesting that the judge take it on their word that they can sue for foreclosure and are counting on homeowners <u>not challenging this position</u>. Unfortunately, few homeowners read the *foreclosure paperwork or hire an attorney to defend them, so they do not realize just how shaky the bank's lawsuit really is.*

This is just one more vitally important reason that homeowners should read the paperwork they are sent by their lenders and challenge everything that seems unfair to them. Especially if the mortgage company is claiming that they have the right to sue but can not prove they have that right, borrowers may wish to consult a contract attorney who can help them defend against the lender's misconduct. Such a legal defense may only stop foreclosure for a short period of time, but it is up to the banks to prove homeowners should lose their homes -- not for homeowners to supplicate themselves at the feet of predatory banks and corrupt judges.

Refer to: http://www.foreclosurefish.com/blog/index.php?id=531

Again, I am not suggesting that you not pay a debt that you lawfully owe. If we borrow money, we should repay it. By the same token, the lender should be upright and not attempt to swindle you out of money and property that they are not entitled to. If neither party keeps their end of the agreement, why should one enjoy restitution[24] at the expense of the other? If both parties breech the agreement, the contract becomes void and of no consequence. It is unenforceable in any court of law or equity. The problem is that most lawyers are ignorant and do not ask the bank (plaintiff) to produce the actual note/contract. This is because most lawyers are taught how to cheat people. Hence, they are better suited at helping big corporations and "THE STATE." They are not suited to help the common person.

[24] The act of making good or compensating for loss, damage, or injury; indemnification.

THE FRAUD OF MONEY AND BANKING

CHAPTER III.

MIS-CON-CEPTIONS AND STRAWMAN THEORIES

Recently there has been a grand awakening by many people involved in the truth movement. Because this is so, the Unknowns and their puppets are hard at work pumping misinformation into that movement. In this book I will cover a few that deal with the banking and monetary systems in the United States. The first is the idea that the Federal Reserve Bank can lawfully be owned by private individuals, foreign governments, and corporations.

In the previous two chapters I have covered some of the misconceptions. However, this chapter is dedicated to correcting the most common. Now, I do not claim to be the smartest person in the world by any standard. The problem I have with some of these misconceptions is the fact that most are taught by people who have no background in the financial world. They have not even taken the time to study the subject. This can easily be noticed in some of the mistakes being made.

Who Owns The Federal Reserve?

Foreigners cannot lawfully own shares in any Federal Reserve district bank. I have read books and have seen documentaries that speak about how foreigners own the Federal Reserve. If banking families (such as the Rothschild's) own shares of the Federal Reserve, they do so by deception. I do not doubt or dispute that this may take place. The frustration is with people who mean well, but are getting mis-information.

We need to do our complete research before we can stand firm on any piece of information. However, you have to always be ready to accept better information than the one you have. This is what a true knowledge seeker does by nature. As I mentioned *supra*, there are books and documentaries which have stated that foreign bankers could own shares of the Federal Reserve. However, foreigners are strictly prohibited from owning the stock of any Federal Reserve Bank. The only way foreigners can own stock is by owning a majority share of the banks that own shares of the Federal Reserve. Even then, banks who own shares in the Federal Reserve only get a 6% preferred stock dividend. And to add to that, the surplus funds of the Federal Reserve go directly to the U. S. Treasury.

The following is from the Federal Reserves own website. The information can also be found under the Federal Reserve Act or title 12 of the United States Code.

> ***What institutions are members of the Federal Reserve System, and what does membership entail?***
>
> ***National banks--those chartered by the federal government (through the Office of the Comptroller of the Currency in the Department of the Treasury)--by law are members of the Federal Reserve System. State- chartered banks and trust companies may apply for membership. To be accepted as a member,***

an applicant must meet requirements set by the Board of Governors.

Member banks must subscribe to stock in their regional Federal Reserve Bank in an amount equal to 6 percent of their capital and surplus, of which 3 percent must be paid in; the remaining 3 percent is subject to call by the Board of Governors. The holding of stock in a Federal Reserve Bank does not carry with it the control and financial interest conveyed to holders of common stock in for-profit organizations. It is merely a legal obligation that goes along with membership, and the stock may not be sold or pledged as collateral for loans. Member banks annually receive a 6 percent dividend on their stock, as specified by law, and vote for some of the directors (so-called class A and class B directors) of their Reserve Bank.

***Source*: http://www.federalreserveeducation.org/FRED/faq/faq.cfm (What institutions are members of the Federal Reserve System, and what does membership entail?)**

Ownership of shares in the Federal Reserve is a requirement of membership to the system. Banks that are members of the Federal Reserve System are required by law to invest 3% of their paid-in capital[25] in a Federal Reserve district bank. The amount of their subscription is set. A bank can own no more or less than the amount allowed by law. In addition, the shares do not confer any rights of ownership beyond the par value of the stock, which is set to $100 per share. Additionally, the Federal Reserve is basically non-profit. The Federal Reserve keeps—in a surplus fund—an amount that is equal to the amount of the

[25] Paid in capital, also known as contributed capital, is the capital a company receives from investors on top of the par value of the stock. Simply stated, any money the company gets from investors over the stated value of the stock is known as paid in capital. For example, if an investor buys shares for $15/share from a company whose stock's par value is stated at $10/share, the companies paid in capital is $5 for each share sold.

member bank's subscriptions. All other earnings are returned to the U.S. Treasury. And, the Federal Reserve IS INDEPENDENTLY AUDITED EVERY YEAR. These audits are part of the Federal Reserve's Annual Report to Congress. Why do people in the truth movement continue to believe that the Federal Reserve has never been independently audited? From the feds own website;

Are the Federal Reserve System and Reserve Banks ever audited?

The Board of Governors, the Federal Reserve Banks, and the Federal Reserve System as a whole are all subject to several levels of audit and review. Under the Federal Banking Agency Audit Act (enacted in 1978 as Public Law 95-320), which authorizes the Comptroller General of the United States to audit the Federal Reserve System, the Government Accountability Office (GAO) has conducted numerous reviews of Federal Reserve activities. In addition, the Board's Office of Inspector General (OIG) audits and investigates Board programs and operations as well as those Board functions delegated to the Reserve Banks. Completed and active GAO reviews and completed OIG audits, reviews, and assessments are listed in the Board's Annual Report (before 2002, the reviews were listed in the Board's Annual Report: Budget Review). The Board's financial statements, and its compliance with laws and regulations affecting those statements, are audited annually by an outside auditor retained by the OIG. The financial statements of the Reserve Banks are also audited annually by an independent outside auditor. In addition, the Reserve Banks are subject to annual examination by the Board. The Board's financial statements and the combined financial statements for the Reserve Banks are published in the Board's Annual Report.

***Sources*: http://www.federalreserve.gov/boarddocs/rptcongress/**
http://www.federalreserve.gov/boarddocs/rptcongress/
http://www.federalreserve.gov/generalinfo/faq/faqfrs.htm#5
[12 USC 248b. As added by act of Nov. 12, 1999 (113 Stat. 1475)]

The Government Accounting Office[26] (herein after GOA) does audit the Federal Reserve. However, the correct argument relating to the GOA's auditing authority against the Federal Reserve should be concentrated on the following facts. Firstly, the law does not provide for the Fed Banks to be audited where transactions with foreign central banks, foreign governments, or discount window operations are concerned. These are probably the largest financial transactions that should be audited. The problem is that the GOA's auditing authority is not expansive. This fatal flaw rests at the feet of Congress. It is the responsibility of our elected congressmen (and women) to amend any laws that are a detriment to the people—especially laws that they themselves have passed!

According to the GOA's own website, their mission is as follows: *"To support the Congress in meeting its constitutional responsibilities and to help improve the performance and ensure the accountability of the federal government for the benefit of the American people. We provide Congress with timely information that is objective, fact-based, non-partisan, non-ideological, fair, and balanced."*

***Source*: http://www.gao.gov/about/index.html**

In the August of 1981, the GOA replied to a letter written by former Assistant Majority Leader of the United States Senate, Mr. Ted Stevens. These letters reveal the limited auditing authority that the GOA has over the Federal Reserve System. It is this limited auditing power that should be the center of the audit argument against the Federal Reserve. Patriots and others need to stop arguing that the fed has NEVER been audited!

---

[26] The U.S. Government Accountability Office (GAO) is an independent, nonpartisan agency that works for Congress. Often called the "Congressional watchdog," GAO investigates how the federal government spends taxpayer dollars. The head of GAO, the Comptroller General of the United States, is appointed to a 15-year term by the president from a slate of candidates Congress proposes.

Former Alaska Senator Ted Stevens, who was convicted eight days before the election of 08' on seven felony counts of violating federal ethics laws for failing to report tens of thousands of dollars in gifts and services he had received from friends, lost his bid for a seventh term as final ballots were counted on November 18.

19123

COMPTROLLER GENERAL OF THE UNITED STATES
WASHINGTON D.C. 20548

B-203576

AUG 10 1981

The Honorable Ted Stevens
Assistant Majority Leader
United States Senate

Dear Senator Stevens:

This responds to your request of May 28, 1981, for our views on H.R. 2322. H.R. 2322 would authorize and direct the General Accounting Office (GAO) to audit the Federal Reserve Board, the Federal Advisory Council, the Federal Open Market Committee, and Federal Reserve banks and their branches. The bill would broaden GAO's authority to audit the Federal Reserve System.

Under present law, GAO's authority to audit the System's economic, monetary, and central bank activities is limited. Specifically, the Accounting and Auditing Act of 1950, as amended by Public Law 95-320 (31 U.S.C. §67(e)), provides that GAO audits of the Federal Reserve System shall not include:

"(A) transactions conducted on behalf of or with foreign central banks, foreign governments, and nonprivate international financing organizations;

"(B) deliberations, decisions, and actions on monetary policy matters, including discount window operations, reserves of member banks, securities credit, interest on deposits, and open market operations;

"(C) transactions made under the direction of the Federal Open Market Committee including transactions of the Federal Reserve System Open Market Account; and

"(D) those portions of oral, written, telegraphic, or telephonic discussions and communications among or between Members of the Board of Governors, and officers and employees of the Federal Reserve System which deal with topics

[Views on H.R. 2322; A Bill Authorizing GAO To Audit The Federal Reserve Board]
017881

listed in subparagraphs (A), (B), and (C) of this paragraph." 31 U.S.C. §67(e)(3).

In effect, these provisions place significant limitations on our ability to audit the Federal Reserve's largest categories of financial transactions and assets. When the matter of GAO's audit responsibility for the Federal Reserve System as a whole was discussed in 1977, we stated in testimony that we did not see how we could satisfactorily audit the Federal Reserve System without authority to examine open market transactions. If the Congress now believes GAO should undertake comprehensive audits of the Federal Reserve's monetary, central bank, and economic functions, an authorization comparable to that contained in H.R. 2322 would be necessary to give us access to the nonpublic data and transaction records that are maintained by the Federal Reserve.

As presently drafted, however, H.R. 2322 contains several ambiguities and omissions that should be addressed in any legislation that would expand our authority to audit the Federal Reserve. The bill does not amend or repeal specifically the audit restrictions contained in existing law. If legislation to expand our audit authority is considered, we suggest that the Accounting and Auditing Act of 1950 be amended to avoid interpretive ambiguities and inconsistencies in our audit and access to records authority.

On a related matter, H.R. 2322 contains no explicit restrictions on the disclosure of confidential information obtained during our audits. This contrasts sharply with the requirements of present law. See 31 U.S.C. §67(e)(5). We recommend that the disclosure prohibitions and safeguards contained in existing law be extended to cover confidential information obtained in connection with audits of the type contemplated by H.R. 2322.

Section (a) of H.R. 2322 requires GAO to audit the named entities at least once each fiscal year. We recommend that the mandatory annual audit requirement be deleted and that the Comptroller General be given the flexibility to determine the frequency of the audit work to be performed. This would be consistent with the discretion provided in present law. As is the case for audits of most Federal agencies, our judgments as to the frequency of the audit work to be performed are made considering congressional requests and interests in specific activities as well as issues, questions, or problems that might surface.

Section (a) of the bill also would require GAO to audit "transactions of the system open market account conducted through recognized dealers." The phrase "conducted through recognized dealers" appears to represent one category of open market account transactions. To the best of our knowledge, however, the term "recognized dealers" is not an official term of the trade, and its meaning could become the subject of confusion. If Congress desires GAO to audit transactions in this area, we suggest that the term "recognized dealer" be defined.

Subsection (b) of H.R. 2322 grants GAO access to the records of the entities subject to audit and requires that GAO "* * * be afforded full facilities for verifying transactions with balances or securities held by depositaries, fiscal agents, and custodians of such entities." Although this seems to authorize GAO direct access to the records of certain financial institutions such as insured commercial banks, present law prohibits GAO from conducting onsite examinations of open insured banks and bank holding companies without the written consent of the appropriate regulatory agency. To avoid confusion regarding the relationship between this restriction and the access authorization contained in H.R. 2322, we recommend that the circumstances under which GAO can obtain direct access to records of financial institutions, including insured commercial banks, be clarified, and that the terms "depositaries, fiscal agents, and custodians" be defined.

Section (c) of H.R. 2322 requires GAO's reports to the Congress to show any activity observed during the course of the audit which in the Comptroller General's opinion was carried out without authority of law. We view this provision as unnecessary since it is already a basic responsibility and policy of this Office to ascertain whether programs subject to our review authority are performed in accordance with law and to report such matters to the appropriate agencies and to the Congress.

We recognize that changes in GAO's audit authority with respect to the Federal Reserve System involve complex considerations. We appreciate this opportunity to express our views on H.R. 2322, and we will be pleased to provide whatever additional information you might require. We are sending copies of this letter to chairmen of the appropriate congressional committees and to Congressman Paul, the sponsor of the bill. We will also make copies available to others on request.

Sincerely yours,

MILTON J. SOCOLAR

Acting Comptroller General
of the United States

The Structure Of The Federal Reserve System

If it appears that I am defending or speaking on behalf of the Federal Reserve Banking System, I am not. My goal is to shatter some of the myths that are hurting people who have relied on them. Again I repeat, stop using these myths and misconceptions. There are many phonies who have infiltrated the truth movement. These phonies have you back to square one. By that I mean; they have you believing things again. We do not need any more beliefs. We need facts! We need tangible information. Truth seekers need to get away from arguments that will take them nowhere—even if they win the argument. For instance, who cares if the Federal Reserve is a private corporation? It is an immaterial argument because the profits go directly to the United States Treasury. If someone has evidence to the contrary, it should be presented. They need to file a lawsuit or contact their local authorities. Otherwise, why are we in this battle against the Unknowns? We will never win that battle with non-sensical ideas and theories. This is why we should strive to know. There are three things that could instantly shift the balance of power in the United States or any country on the planet.

1. Knowledge of how the Government works (the role of Government).
2. Knowledge of economics
3. Knowledge of law

An uninformed person will do anything that they are instructed to do. This is especially true when instructed by someone they trust or believe is of a superior intellect. My goal is to direct your attention toward relying on facts (only). Do not rely on charisma or nice colorful words. The following is also directly from the feds own website.

The Federal Reserve Board

The Structure of the Federal Reserve System

Federal Reserve Banks

Organization of the Banks

Federal Reserve Banks operate under the general supervision of the Board of Governors in Washington. Each Bank has a nine-member Board of Directors that oversees its operations.

Federal Reserve Banks generate their own income, primarily from interest earned on government securities that are acquired in the course of Federal Reserve monetary policy actions. A secondary source of income is derived from the provision of priced services to depository institutions, as required by the Monetary Control Act of 1980. Federal Reserve Banks are not, however, operated for a profit, and each year they return to the U.S. Treasury all earnings in excess of Federal Reserve operating and other expenses.

***Source*: http://www.federalreserve.gov/pubs/frseries/frseri3.htm**

The workings of the banking system are purposely kept from the people. It is not widely taught at any level of education. Only those who major in business and finance have a clue. However, even they are taught a corrupt form of the system. This is done intentionally to assist the banking gangsters in their corruption and total takeover of our lives. This ignorance has even spread into the truth movement. I cannot stress this enough. Many books and lectures about the banking fraud have been giving false information. One of the prominent falsehoods state that if Frank (using the example found at *supra*) deposits $100 in the bank, the bank may lend $1,000. This is incorrect information. Banks do not have the lawful authority to print Federal Reserve notes (money). Where would the other $900 come from when the loan check for the $1,000 is cashed? If a bank performed this type of fraud, it would go under in less than a year.

When Frank deposits $100 in the bank, the banks accounting department creates three accounts. This is how Frank's transaction appears on the banks balance sheet.

	(asset) Debit	Credit (liability)
(Reserve account)	$10	$100 (Franks Account)
(Excess Reserve Account)	$90	

The bank's balance sheet will show Frank's account as a liability, and it will post the reserve account and excess reserve account as an asset.[27]

If the bank received a $100 deposit from Frank, where on the ledger would the bank put the $900? If audited, how would the bank account for the extra $900? Also, why would the bank stop at lending only $900? Why not lend $9,000?

Who creates the money? Does the bank create the money, or do the depositors and borrowers create the money? This idea that Frank's deposit of $100 allows the bank to loan $1,000 would mean the bank is committing a fraud in violation of its charter, including state and federal banking laws. It has become common for people to accept these misconceptions about fractional reserve banking and

[27] Note that the names of these accounts may differ from bank to bank.

how money is actually created. Some even suggest that the Federal Reserve prints an obscene amount of money. This is another falsehood. The Federal Reserve does not print money! All money is printed by the Bureau of Engraving and Printing. Any of the 12 member banks of the Federal Reserve may obtain currency from the Bureau of Engraving and Printing, but it must pay the cost of producing the currency. The cost of this production becomes a liability for the Federal Reserve Banks. In addition, they cannot just keep ordering money from the Bureau of Engraving and Printing whenever they feel like it. If a member bank orders one million dollars in Federal Reserve notes, it must hold collateral equal in value to the Federal Reserve notes the bank receives, i.e., gold certificates, silver certificates and/or United States securities. Unfortunately for us, the notes are collateralized with United States securities and commercial paper, as Federal Reserve banks receive the commercial paper as collateral from commercial banks. Once upon a time, Federal Reserve notes were redeemable in lawful money, payable to the bearer on demand.

1928 series $10 Federal Reserve note

The bearer of this 1928 series $10 Federal Reserve note could redeem a gold or silver certificate worth $10. So, does the Federal Reserve print money? No! It does not. We need to stop this non-sense. This type of information has hurt many people in the truth movement. Many people have attempted to defend their money and property in court using these frivolous arguments and have been slaughtered by the enemy. These types of frivolous arguments make intelligent people in banking (those who would normally help in this struggle) turn their backs on us. They hear the frivolous information and write us off as ignorant fools who do not understand how money or the banking profession works.

Another common misconception is the one which stipulates that the federal government owes most of its debt to the Federal Reserve Bank because it borrows Federal Reserve notes (money). This is wrong knowledge. The United States Treasury Department issues securities or IOUs, such as Treasury bills, Treasury notes, and Treasury bonds. When lenders buy these securities, the money goes to the federal government. In return, the government pays interest to the owners of the securities. Some Treasury notes are paid interest at maturity.

Who are these owners? Again, there is an understanding within the truth movement that the owners of these securities are the wealthy banking families of Europe. Although this may be the case, they are not owned out right. They are owned by and through foreign banks, corporations, and governments that they (banking families) control. However, as a means to loosen the money supply, the FOMC orders the purchase of United States Government securities. These securities are purchased by the Federal Reserve Banks. Keep in mind, however, that the Federal Reserve Bank turns over its excess revenues to the U.S. Treasury. So again, even if the Federal Reserve Banks are holding most U.S. Government debt (52% as of Dec 31, 2007), they cannot benefit from that debt. Foreign governments and corporations owned about 25% of U.S. Government debt as of Dec 31, 2007.

The argument that the Rothschild's or foreign banking families own the Federal Reserve is unsubstantiated given this data. If they do own the Federal Reserve, they do so by way of subterfuge or some other stratagem. What many of us fail to realize is that the Bretton Woods system of monetary management established the rules for commercial and financial relations for the world's major industrial nations.

This means that you do not have to try and qualify that the Rothschild banking empire owns the Federal Reserve. The Federal Reserve is a creature of the International Monetary Fund and the World Bank. (More on that later).

Below is a quick graph of the top 16 foreign owners of U.S. Government securities.

MAJOR FOREIGN HOLDERS OF TREASURY SECURITIES
(in billions of dollars)
HOLDINGS 1/ AT END OF PERIOD

Country	Aug 2008	Jul 2008	Jun 2008	May 2008	Apr 2008	Mar 2008	Feb 2008	Jan 2008	Dec 2007	Nov 2007	Oct 2007	Sep 2007	Aug 2007
Japan	585.9	593.4	583.8	578.7	592.2	600.7	586.6	586.9	581.2	590.9	601.7	591.9	595.8
China, Mainland	541.0	518.7	503.8	506.8	502.0	490.6	486.9	492.6	477.6	458.9	459.1	467.7	471.2
United Kingdom 2/	307.4	291.5	280.4	272.5	247.8	201.1	181.1	161.9	158.2	174.3	155.0	120.3	99.8
Oil Exporters 3/	179.8	173.9	170.4	164.3	153.9	150.8	146.1	140.9	137.9	138.7	141.6	137.1	134.7
Carib Bnkng Ctrs 4/	147.7	133.7	122.4	104.7	115.4	107.1	103.0	108.1	116.7	107.4	105.6	99.1	103.8
Brazil	146.2	148.4	151.6	151.4	149.5	149.1	146.6	141.7	129.9	121.7	113.9	110.5	107.7
Luxembourg	77.5	75.8	88.6	80.4	84.8	92.7	83.1	68.4	69.7	68.3	63.3	58.4	57.1
Russia	74.4	74.1	65.3	63.7	60.2	42.4	38.4	35.2	32.7	33.5	33.6	31.8	31.9
Hong Kong	61.2	60.6	61.2	61.4	63.2	60.6	57.5	54.4	51.2	51.7	51.3	52.6	53.2
Switzerland	45.3	45.1	44.4	42.1	42.5	41.2	39.4	39.3	38.9	38.1	37.8	37.0	37.4
Germany	41.5	41.1	40.9	45.0	43.7	42.2	42.2	42.7	41.7	39.1	41.8	41.8	42.3
Norway	41.3	41.8	43.3	47.1	45.3	44.5	34.0	33.6	26.2	27.6	25.5	22.9	6.4
Taiwan	40.6	42.3	40.9	40.1	42.6	41.2	38.8	38.9	38.2	37.1	40.7	39.9	39.5
Korea	37.9	35.3	36.5	38.5	40.5	40.7	41.4	42.1	39.2	37.8	37.0	39.4	42.6
Turkey	34.0	32.4	30.3	28.9	31.1	28.7	28.5	28.2	25.6	25.6	28.1	28.3	29.2
Mexico	33.5	36.0	42.5	40.4	38.0	38.8	36.5	35.6	34.5	32.0	30.5	30.0	30.2

***Source*: http://www.treas.gov/tic/mfh.txt**

Japan and China are the biggest purchasers of U.S. Government securities. Since 1999, China has been the busiest purchaser of U.S. Government securities. This basically means that China has been one of the biggest financiers of the United States Federal Government. As China continues to become an industrial juggernaut, the United States continues to get closer to a third world status. Factories in the United States continue to close and farmers continue to dwindle. For the working class people of the United States, this only spells more trouble in the foreseeable future. The most troubling issue with China becoming one of the biggest financiers of the United States Government is that the new administration, under Barack Obama and his top advisor Zbigniew Brzezinski, has always had an itch to war with Russia. This is troubling because it is a known fact that Russia and China currently maintain close and cordial diplomatic relations, strong geopolitical and regional cooperation, and significant levels of trade. And now that lord Obama is in office, the relationship between the United States and China has suddenly dipped south.

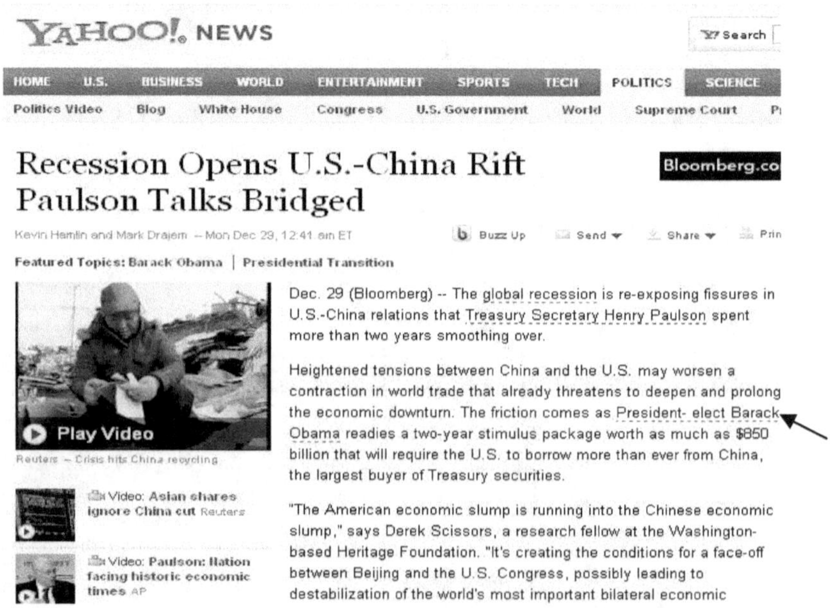
YAHOO! NEWS

Search

HOME U.S. BUSINESS WORLD ENTERTAINMENT SPORTS TECH POLITICS SCIENCE

Politics Video Blog White House Congress U.S. Government World Supreme Court

Bloomberg.co

Recession Opens U.S.-China Rift Paulson Talks Bridged

Kevin Hamlin and Mark Drajem -- Mon Dec 29, 12:41 am ET

Buzz Up Send Share Prin

Featured Topics: Barack Obama | Presidential Transition

Play Video

Reuters -- Crisis hits China recycling

Video: Asian shares ignore China cut Reuters

Video: Paulson: Nation facing historic economic times AP

Dec. 29 (Bloomberg) -- The global recession is re-exposing fissures in U.S.-China relations that Treasury Secretary Henry Paulson spent more than two years smoothing over.

Heightened tensions between China and the U.S. may worsen a contraction in world trade that already threatens to deepen and prolong the economic downturn. The friction comes as President- elect Barack Obama readies a two-year stimulus package worth as much as $850 billion that will require the U.S. to borrow more than ever from China, the largest buyer of Treasury securities.

"The American economic slump is running into the Chinese economic slump," says Derek Scissors, a research fellow at the Washington-based Heritage Foundation. "It's creating the conditions for a face-off between Beijing and the U.S. Congress, possibly leading to destabilization of the world's most important bilateral economic

Setting The Record Straight

There are many arguments and ideas used by patriots and truth seekers concerning money and banking. Many of these arguments and theories have been referred to as Patriot Mythology by some who are trying to also set the record straight.

1. Banks create money out of thin air

The most common argument is that banks create money out of thin air. As stated in Frank's example, money is created out of nothing, but the banks do not create this money on their own. It is this debt based[28] economy that brings it about. Money is created by borrowers and depositors. We cannot go into court and claim that we do not have to pay our loan because the bank created the money out of thin air. Remember, you exchanged cash (M1) for a negotiable instrument (M3). The fraud comes in when you get the short end of the stick in the deal. For starters, you are paying interest on your side (M1) and they are not. When the contract is completed and you have returned the money (M1) to the bank, you are entitled to your M3. If the bank cannot produce the original note, they are committing fraud. Out of ignorance, people are accepting copies of their mortgage or car notes at maturity. Do you believe the bank would accept (as payment of the loan) copies of Federal Reserve notes? Then why should you receive a copy of your M3?

---

[28] Most mainstream economist would refer to our monetary system as "Credit based" rather than "Debt based". All-in-all, it equals the same concept. They are just looking from the banker's side (creditor) and not form the borrower's side (debtor).

2. When you borrow money from a banking institution, you are financing your own loan.

This goes hand in hand with the previous example. Again, there is some truth to it; but only in the sense that you are creating the M3 by putting your signature on that paper (note). A more proper term would be to say that you are funding your own loan by creating an unmatured asset (M3-negotiable instrument) and exchanging it for M1 (cash). The loan is actually financed by the bank from its *excess reserves* (its customer's money/deposits).

3. The National Debt is owed to the Federal Reserve Bank.

Once again, this is only partly true. The government owes roughly forty percent of the national debt to itself through the Federal Reserve Bank and other government accounts. However, keep in mind that the Federal Reserve forwards its excess revenue to the Treasury Department after it has paid for expenses.

The remainder of the debt is owed to foreign investors, insurance companies, banks, and other privately held entities. The money is used to operate the federal government, which (as of the date of this writing) currently costs well over two trillion dollars a year.

The debt is the total amount of money owed by the government, and the deficit is the yearly amount by which the government outspends itself. Most of the misconceptions about the Federal Reserve can be dispelled by simply reading the Federal Reserve Act. (Refer to appendix B of this book)

4. A Federal Reserve note is a counterfeit currency not worth anything

According to Merriam Webster's Dictionary, the word counterfeit means: *Made in imitation of something else with intent to deceive*. This does not fit the description of a Federal Reserve note because the face of the note informs the holder of the following: (1.) It is a note. (2.) It is legal tender; meaning a lawful medium of exchange (3) and lastly, it is for all debts—public and private. Whoever attempts to copy its contents become the counterfeiters. A Federal Reserve note could only be considered a counterfeit currency if it is an imitation that is made with the intent to deceptively represent the content or origin of another.

It is humorous that the people who say Federal Reserve notes are worthless will use them as a medium of exchange. In Medieval England, tally sticks became a medium of exchange (money) because the English Government accepted the tally sticks as a form of payment for taxes. Naturally, people traded the tally sticks for goods and services. How much would you pay, or what would you give up for some tally sticks today? Nothing! Why? Because you can no longer exchange them for anything of value. As long as people continue to exchange Federal Reserve notes for things of value, they will be worth something (i.e. whatever you exchange for them).

I believe people confuse the fact that Federal Reserve notes are not backed or redeemable in gold or silver, with being worthless. If you buy an expensive bicycle, is it worthless because you cannot redeem the bicycle for anything of value (i.e. gold or silver)? The bike shop is not going to exchange your bike for anything other than Federal Reserve notes or perhaps a bicycle of equal value. If you ask the bike shop to give you gold or silver for the bicycle, they might think you are insane. However, the bicycle is not worthless because you may still exchange it for cash or other goods—as long as there is a market (someone willing to buy) for your bicycle. The same thing happens with Federal Reserve notes. As long as someone is willing to exchange goods or services for Federal Reserve notes, they will be worth something. But who in their right minds would exchange paper for goods and services? I will tell you what person. Any person who can pay their taxes with that paper.

THE FRAUD OF MONEY AND BANKING

CHAPTER IV.

"PROMISES TO PAY vs. REAL MONEY"

What is a promise to pay as opposed to actual money? To clearly understand the difference, you must understand the history of real money. Today, money is considered a commodity for different reasons than it did in antiquity. In the olden days, people accepted goods and services in exchange for other goods and services they lacked. If you needed bananas or apples, you might purchase them with rice, beans, or anything you owned an abundance of. This system is commonly referred to as a barter system. Once the products become universally accepted as a medium of exchange, the products become a standard of value as a result of being continually compared to other commodities.

It can be said that people once grew their own money. Among the things used as money by many people throughout history are; wheat, rice, beans, salt, silk, tobacco, fish, fur, olive oil, cotton, iron, copper, nickel, silver, and gold. During the American colonial period, the established colonial governments passed laws to fix the prices of certain commodities. In July of 1619, the first

General Assembly of Virginia met at Jamestown to enact certain laws. The first law passed was one fixing the price of tobacco. Once upon a time tobacco was considered to be the currency of the colony. In 1642, they took it a step further by enacting a law which made tobacco the only medium of exchange.[29] What would you do if you could grow money? Does money grow on trees? It did once upon a time. However, commodities that are liable to great and sudden changes of supply are not a desirable form of money. This happened with the tobacco of Virginia and several other colonies. The cultivation of tobacco increased so rapidly that it caused a sharp drop in the price of tobacco. In the year 1666, a treaty was signed into law between the colonies of Virginia, Maryland, and Carolina to stop planting tobacco for one whole year.[30] The goal was to raise the price of tobacco.

In 1727, tobacco notes were issued by official inspectors. These notes became certificates of deposit in government warehouses. It is the same concept as the goldsmiths and the gold receipts. These tobacco notes became lawful money and were payable for all tobacco debts. The tobacco in the warehouses was the real medium of exchange (money). The tobacco notes were orders payable to the bearer. Anything payable to the bearer is a promise to pay. The difference between real money and "a promise to pay" money is the same difference between a meal and a meal ticket. The meal is the actual money and the meal ticket is a promise made by the maker of the ticket that you will get a meal upon demand. Therefore, the meal ticket is equivalent to a bearer note or bearer bond.

---

[29] The act of 1642 was repealed in 1656, but nearly all of the trading continued to be made with tobacco as the medium.

[30] The same thing was done during the great depression; with the introduction of the Agricultural Adjustment Act of 1933, the government attempted to stabilize crop prices by controlling the supply.

A common measure of value

Money is usually defined as a common measure of value, a medium of exchange, and a standard of deferred payments. The value of any type of money depends upon how often it is used and whether the people see it as something of value. In order to inject value into any government issued currency, the government makes all taxes payable in the issuing currency. This gives their money instant credibility and worth.

The word "money" is derived from the Latin *monēre* (which means to remind, warn, or instruct). Later it was grafted into the word *moneta*. In the Spanish language (which is a dialect of Latin), we have the word *moneda* translated to mean money. However, the more common term for money in the Spanish language is *dinero*. The term "*dinero*" was the name of the currency used by the Christian states of Spain during the Muslim Moorish rule of the eleventh century AD. The term *moneta* was first used during Roman times at the temple of Hera. In the Greek Pantheon of gods and goddesses, Hera is the equivalent to the Roman Goddess Juno Moneta. The temple of Hera (*moneta*) was located on a hill called "*Capitoline*." If you are a coincidence lover, then you will believe the coincidence that in Washington DC there is a "Capitol Hill." The word "capital" or "capitol" can also be applied to the amount of wealth a person or corporation (by law the same) controls or is capable of controlling.

Today, most people do not have the slightest idea of what money is. They do not know any technical terms such as M1, M2, or fiat currency. When people hear those terms, they get confused by so many definitions of the money supply. Nearly every single working family in the United States has a bank account. And yet, most working families do not have a clue as to how the banking world operates. We are purposely kept ignorant so that we do not question being defrauded and robbed. They have purposely created complicated rules and regulations to make sure you keep your distance from the game. They know that you are pre-occupied with the daily dealings of your life. Therefore, they count on the fact that you do not have the time or the means to dive into the corrupt world of banking. In order to keep things this way, they make sure that words and phrases are never succinct.[31] Mortgage brokers, bank tellers, and others in the banking field are in most cases as ignorant as the layperson.[32] These people are the middle-men between you and the bank. But have you ever tried asking any of them a technical question? They usually do not know—but they are not supposed to know. This is all part of the compartmentalization plan that the criminal elite always have in place. They always have us sectioned off into parts. This is why there is practically nothing that the public will not buy into.[33] We easily buy into the inflation[34] fraud. When we go into a store and notice a rise in prices, we immediately accuse the greedy merchant for wanting more profits. We do not understand that the number one cause of inflation is the increase of the money supply absent an equal increase in goods and services. The government (which has produced the inflation with its exuberant borrowing) uses economists and other financial cronies to pass the blame onto the manufacturers and merchants. And as always, the politicians take on the role of the heroes fighting for lower costs.

---

[31] Succinct is defined as; being explained by compact precise expression without wasted words.

[32] A person who is not a member of a given profession, such as law, banking, or medicine. It may also refer to an average person.

[33] I would like to note that most people (although they did not understand the bill) did not want the $700 billion banker bailout bill.

[34] Economists use the term "Inflation" to denote an ongoing rise in the general level of prices quoted in units of money. With U.S. dollar prices rising, a one-dollar bill buys less each year. Inflation is thus defined as an ongoing fall in the overall purchasing power of the monetary unit.

Colonial Script

Before I break down the fraud of today's monetary system, it is important to note that even though paper money has become the main measure of value for almost everything these days, I understand its benefits. I recognize that the problem with money is how it is used and perceived in the minds of the people. I recognize that it is not the actual existence of paper money that is the cause of our problems—or as they say, "The root of all evil." Another thing that should be noted here as well is that money should not be created through legislature. Money should always get its instructions from a free market. The monetary system should be a system designed to make the trade in goods, ideas, and services easier. If money was used only in this capacity, it would not create the massive inequalities in wealth distribution that we see today. The economic practice of usury and the abuse of fractional reserve banking have become harmful triggers of the current monetary system. Others argue that the biggest problem is fiat currency.

Although I am not a big cheerleader of fiat currency, keep in mind that Colonial Script was a form of fiat currency. However, it worked great for the colonies that created money based on the credit of that colonial government and on the goods and services available in their economy. Since it was the colonial governments that were issuing the money, they were able to charge low interest when the people borrowed money. The income earned from the interest lowered the tax burden on the people. This, in turn, contributed to even greater prosperity.

Because Colonial script was not backed by gold or silver, the colonies could control its purchasing power. This was similar to the old "tally stick" system used by the British. Colonial Script was in contrast to what the European Governments were doing. The European Governments were totally dependant on the big banks (namely the House Of Rothschild) to issue currency and set monetary policy. This was the common theme in the mercantilist system of money set up by the European banking families. Needles to say, the European bankers were not amused with the money system that was being implemented by the colonies.[35] The Bank of England (in particular) saw Colonial Script as a threat to their monetary system.

The Colonial Scripts were actually bills of credit created by the colonial governments based on their own credit. There was no interest to pay any bank for its creation. Therefore, the colonial governments did not have to bare the burden of the expense to bring money into circulation. This allowed the colonial governments to charge the people low interest rates when the script was loaned. All the positives that came from the issuance of Colonial Script contributed to the prosperity of the colonies during the era of the script. Taxing the people was never an issue because taxes would only be raised when the notes became excessive in the economy. The raising of taxes retired the excess scripts out of circulation. This helped the colonies avoid long periods of inflation. Unfortunately, the *Currency Act* that was passed by the English Parliament in 1764 ordered the colonies to discontinue issuing Colonial Script or any type of paper currency.

Benjamin Franklin stated in his autobiography that the passing of the *Currency Act* of 1764 was the main cause of the Revolutionary War. Strangely enough, it was Franklin who went to England and began boasting of the success that Colonial script was having on the colonial economy.

Peter Cooper, founder of Cooper Union College, Vice-President of the New York Board of Currency, and U.S. Presidential Candidate in 1876, said the following in his 1883 book entitled; *Ideas for a Science of Good Government*:

> ***After Franklin had explained...to the British Government as the real cause of***

[35] Not all colonial governments that issued scrip were successful.

prosperity, they immediately passed laws, forbidding the payment of taxes in that money. This produced such great inconvenience and misery to the people, that it was the principal cause of the Revolution. A far greater reason for a general uprising, than the Tea and Stamp Act, was the taking away of the paper money.

Benjamin Franklin
October 18, 1785 – December 1, 1788

Colonial Script is the best argument used for having a fiat currency. However, as I have previously stated, it may be irrelevant whether we have a fiat or specie currency. The most important thing is to match the currency with the demand for that currency. In other words, allow supply and demand to dictate the amount of currency in circulation. Federal Reserve notes are inflated because its issuance is out of control. The notes are being issued according to debt and not according to the amount of goods and services in the economy.

Earlier I stated that Federal Reserve notes were not counterfeit because they are not copies or imitations of any other currencies. However, this does not mean that the notes are excused from being deceitful. For one thing, Federal Reserve notes no longer contain a redemption clause. Thus, Federal Reserve banks are not obligated to redeem their notes. If you go to any Federal Reserve bank and ask to have your paper money exchanged for lawful money, they can comply or they can flat out refuse. Why? Because the note (dollar) you have in your pocket does not promise to pay anything to the bearer. Keep in mind, a note is an IOU. The Federal Reserve banks issuing the dollars that you have in your pocket are not legally obligated to honor their debts (Fed notes). Also remember, that in order to have the Bureau of Engraving and Printing print their notes, all the fed banks need to do is put up government securities or commercial paper[36] as collateral.

The dollars we use today should really be called labor certificates. They have no intrinsic value. The only value is the promise that the United States Government will accept them as payment of taxes. How does the government get taxes? They get them from our labor. Both personal income taxes and excise taxes are created by the labor of the people. Today Federal Reserve notes are really a form of script in which taxes are levied. This may sound strange or confusing to the average person, but imagine if the government accepted something other than Federal Reserve dollars as payment for taxes. Using the old Tally Stick system, let us say the government began to accept Tally Sticks as payment for taxes. Federal Reserve

---

[36] They may also put up gold or silver certificates. However, most of these certificates were U.S. notes that were discontinued in 1968. The Riegle Community Development and Regulatory Improvement Act, Public Law 103-325, codified at 31 U.S.C. 5119(b)(2), enacted in September 1994, amended 31 U.S.C. by canceling the requirement to reissue these notes when they are redeemed.

dollars would lose most of their value. Why? Because people would inevitably begin to trade Tally Sticks for value during commercial transactions. This would decrease the demand for Federal Reserve notes. The old silver and gold certificates were the reasons why the Federal Reserve had to back the old Federal Reserve notes with some type of intrinsic value. Between 1914 and 1934, most Federal Reserve notes read, "REDEEMABLE IN GOLD ON DEMAND AT THE UNITED STATES TREASURY OR IN GOLD OR LAWFUL MONEY AT ANY FEDERAL RESERVE BANK." The lawful money at the time was gold and silver certificates issued by the United States Treasury.

On April 5, 1933, President Franklin Delano Roosevelt declared Presidential Executive Order 6102 the law. This order basically made it unlawful for the people to own lawful money in gold. From 1934 to 1963, Federal Reserve Notes read; THIS NOTE IS LEGAL TENDER FOR ALL DEBTS PUBLIC AND PRIVATE AND IS REDEEMABLE IN LAWFUL MONEY AT THE UNITED STATES TREASURY OR ANY FEDERAL RESERVE BANK. Do you notice that the "REDEEMABLE IN GOLD" was removed? This was because you were no longer allowed to own gold. Lawful money at this point was only the silver certificates issued by the U.S. Treasury Department.

On December 31, 1974, President Gerald Ford repealed the limitation on gold ownership by signing a bill re-legalizing the private ownership of gold coins and certificates. The bill was codified in Pub.L. 93-373. However, the law did not repeal the *Gold Clause Resolution* of 1933—which states that it is unlawful for anyone to issue, sign, or participate in any contract that specifies payment in a fixed amount of gold. If any contract contained any such provision, the contract would be deemed unenforceable. Gold was to be used only as a commodity trade, but not as a monetary instrument. In other words, it could not be used as money. The banking elite that are in control of the monetary system have always considered gold and silver as the real money. Therefore, in order to maintain the slavery, they had to make sure the slave did not have real money, i.e., gold and silver.

Presidential Executive Order 6102

From: President of the United States Franklin Delano Roosevelt
To: The United States Congress
Dated: 5 April, 1933

(in part)

Forbidding the Hoarding of Gold Coin, Gold Bullion and Gold Certificates By virtue of the authority vested in me by Section 5(b) of the Act of October 6, 1917, as amended by Section 2 of the Act of March 9, 1933, entitled

An Act to provide relief in the existing national emergency in banking, and for other purposes~',

in which amendatory Act Congress declared that a serious emergency exists,

I, Franklin D. Roosevelt, President of the United States of America, do declare that said national emergency still continues to exist and pursuant to said section to do hereby prohibit the hoarding gold coin, gold bullion, and gold certificates within the continental United States by individuals, partnerships, associations and corporations and hereby prescribe the following regulations for carrying out the purposes of the order:

Section 1. For the purpose of this regulation, the term 'hoarding" means the withdrawal and withholding of gold coin, gold bullion, and gold certificates from the recognized and customary channels of trade. The term "person" means any individual, partnership, association or corporation.

Section 2. All persons are hereby required to deliver on or before May 1, 1933, to a Federal Reserve bank or a branch or agency thereof or to any member bank of the Federal Reserve System all gold coin, gold bullion, and gold certificates now owned by them or coming into their ownership on or before April 28, 1933, except the following:

(a) Such amount of gold as may be required for legitimate and customary use in industry, profession or art within a reasonable time, including gold prior to refining and stocks of gold in reasonable amounts for the usual trade requirements of owners mining and refining such gold.

(b) Gold coin and gold certificates in an amount not exceeding in the aggregate $100.00 belonging to any one person; and gold coins having recognized special value to collectors of rare and unusual coins.

(c) Gold coin and bullion earmarked or held in trust for a recognized foreign government or foreign central bank or the Bank for International Settlements.

(d) Gold coin and bullion licensed for the other proper transactions (not involving hoarding) including gold coin and gold bullion imported for the re-export or held pending action on applications for export license.

Section 3. Until otherwise ordered any person becoming the owner of any gold coin, gold bullion, and gold certificates after April 28, 1933, shall within three days after receipt thereof, deliver the same in the manner prescribed in Section 2; unless such gold coin, gold bullion, and gold certificates are held for any of the purposes specified in paragraphs (a),(b) or (c) of Section 2; or unless such gold coin, gold bullion is held for purposes specified in paragraph (d) of Section 2 and the person holding it is, with respect to such gold coin or bullion, a licensee or applicant for license pending action thereon.

Source: http://www.presidency.ucsb.edu/ws/index.php?pid=14611&st=&st1=

The order was also posted in post offices throughout the country by the Postmaster General, James A. Farley. The following page has a copy of that order. This was part of the process of overthrowing the real economy.

In order to introduce their debt-based fiat monetary system, they had to take all of the people's gold and silver (real money) and replace them with fiat legal tender notes. As we learned in high school history class, slaves were not permitted to own money.

POSTMASTER: PLEASE POST IN A CONSPICUOUS PLACE. — JAMES A. FARLEY, Postmaster General

UNDER EXECUTIVE ORDER OF THE PRESIDENT

Issued April 5, 1933

all persons are required to deliver

ON OR BEFORE MAY 1, 1933

all GOLD COIN, GOLD BULLION, AND GOLD CERTIFICATES now owned by them to a Federal Reserve Bank, branch or agency, or to any member bank of the Federal Reserve System.

Executive Order

[illegible]

For Further Information Consult Your Local Bank

GOLD CERTIFICATES may be identified by the words "GOLD CERTIFICATE" appearing thereon. The serial number and the Treasury seal on the face of a GOLD CERTIFICATE are printed in YELLOW. Be careful not to confuse GOLD CERTIFICATES with other issues which are redeemable in gold but which are not GOLD CERTIFICATES. Federal Reserve Notes and United States Notes are "redeemable in gold" but are not "GOLD CERTIFICATES" and are not required to be surrendered

Special attention is directed to the exceptions allowed under Section 2 of the Executive Order

CRIMINAL PENALTIES FOR VIOLATION OF EXECUTIVE ORDER
$10,000 fine or 10 years imprisonment, or both, as provided in Section 9 of the order

Secretary of the Treasury.

Source: **http://www.wellsfargonevadagold.com/confiscation-order.pdf**

A Federal Reserve note is legal tender. However, since it is a note that does not pay anything in particular (i.e., gold or silver), a good question is; to tender what? If you go to a Federal Reserve Bank and try to redeem these notes, they will probably exchange new notes for the ones you attempt to redeem. This basically means that Federal Reserve notes are promises to pay nothing!

The legal foundation of our current fiat monetary system is the legal tender law that is found at 31 U.S.C. § 5103, which states;

> *United States coins and currency (including Federal Reserve notes and circulating notes of Federal Reserve banks and national banks) are legal tender for all debts, public charges, taxes, and dues. Foreign gold or silver coins are not legal tender for debts.*

Refer to: http://www.law.cornell.edu/uscode/31/5103.html

Notice how they were careful to make sure they did not violate article I: section X of the constitution. United States coins are no longer made of either gold or silver (unless specially ordered from the Dept. of Printing & Engraving). It has always been common knowledge that foreign coins, whether gold or silver, were not legal tender. All foreign coins had to be exchanged for lawful money.

State Coinage Clause/State Legal Tender Clause

Article I: Section 10

No State shall enter into any Treaty, Alliance, or Confederation; grant Letters of Marque and Reprisal; coin Money; emit Bills of Credit; make any Thing but gold and silver Coin a Tender in Payment of Debts......

According to the United States Constitution, every state must offer to pay their debts in gold or silver coin. This means that if your state or any state of the union owes you money, you have a legal right to demand payment in gold or silver.

Good Money vs. Bad Money

In order to get a good understanding of the fraud of money and banking, you only need to know the difference between good money and bad money. A banker, merchant, royal agent, and advisor to Queen Elizabeth I, named Thomas Gersham, has been credited with what is commonly known as *Greshams Law*. Gresham's Law is a theory which states that bad money drives good money out of circulation. In ancient and medieval times, bankers, merchants, and even consumers had a tendency to debase coins. They would then assign the debased coin the same value as coins containing greater quantities of precious metals. Federal Reserve notes (bad money), slowly but surely, replaced silver certificates, gold certificates, and United States notes (good money). It is import to know the definition of a note. According to Barron's Educational Series; 5th edition (September 1998): *Dictionary of Finance and Investment terms,* a note is defined as:

> *A written promise to pay a specified amount to a certain entity on demand or on a specified date. See also MUNICIPAL NOTE; PROMISSORY NOTE; TREASURIES.*
>
> *P. 402*

Again, a note is basically an unconditional, writ-ten, signed promise to pay a certain amount of money on demand or at a certain date defined in the future. Therefore, a "note" is evidence of a debt.

Once upon a time, a Federal Reserve note was paid in gold or silver. There were no interests bearing bonds issued to produce the notes (money). This is one of the key reasons why the government did not obtain such a huge debt until after the establishment of the Federal Reserve fiat money became a monopoly. Federal Reserve notes are no longer printed on the presentment of gold. They are printed on the presentment of Treasury bills, Treasury notes, and Treasury bonds.

> U.S. Treasury bills- *Treasury bills, or T-bills, are sold in terms ranging from a few days to 52 weeks. Bills are sold at a discount from their face value. For instance, you might pay $990 for a $1,000 bill. When the bill matures, you would be paid $1,000. The difference between the purchase price and face value is interest.*
> U.S. Treasury notes- *Treasury notes, sometimes called T-Notes, earn a fixed rate of interest every six months until maturity. Notes are issued in terms of 2, 3, 5, and 10 years.*
> U.S. Treasury bonds- *Treasury bonds or T-Bonds also known as the "long bond" have the longest maturity ranging from ten years to thirty years. They have coupon payment every six months like T-Notes, and are commonly issued with maturity of thirty years.*

In essence, the Federal Reserve notes are representing these interest bearing bonds. Who pays this interest? You do! The tax-paying-public gets stuck with the bill. This is why they had to implement the personal income tax. It was set up to pay for this Ponzi scheme. This was all set up in 1913 with the passing of the Federal Reserve Act, the passing of the Sixteenth Amendment (Amendment XVI) to the United States Constitution, and the passing of the United States Revenue Act of 1913—also known as the Tariff Act, Underwood Tariff, or Underwood-Simmons Act (ch. 16, 38 Stat. 116, October 3, 1913). Coincidentally, all of this was taking place in the same year (1913).

The personal income tax that the federal government collects pays for the interest that creates Federal Reserve notes.[37] Making you pay personal income taxes is about control. Any competent economist knows that reliev-

---

[37] Federal Reserve notes (U.S. dollars) must be matched by interest bearing government securities. In other words, when the bureau of Printing and Engraving prints the money, the Federal Reserve must collateralize the amount printed with government securities. This is what is meant by the government borrowing money. It borrows by selling securities that are redeemable with interest.

ing the people from the burden of paying personal income taxes would give the economy a tremendous boost. Simple math says that your paycheck will be of larger amounts. The extra money will, in-turn, enable you to spend more money and save more money. Consumer spending and consumer savings are the essential elements to a healthy economy. However, we are led to believe that our personal income taxes help the government pay for services that benefit us. This is incorrect and an out-right fairy tale. As Representative Ron Paul (R - TX) has stated many times; "How was the government funding itself before 1913?"

In 1982, President Ronald Reagan's administration set up the *Private Sector Survey on Cost Control*, or the *PSSCC*, commonly known as *The Grace Commission*. The Grace Commission revealed that 100% of your personal income tax revenue is used up to pay the interest on the national debt before any of it is used for any government services (refer to appendix d). Maybe this is why the government does not do anything for the people. When the people stop paying the government to spend money, the people might get somewhere. Until then, keep allowing them to spend your money (labor) on projects that keep you in debt slavery.

Even though the following article was published over 18 years ago, the government has continually ignored all the recommendations made by the Grace Commission's report. Can we get a grip on the reality that every personal income tax dollar they collect vanishes before any of it is disbursed to serve the people? Once that sinks into your head, think about all the excuses politicians and other criminals use to enforce the personal income tax through the barrel of a gun. I say the barrel of a gun because if you refuse to pay, they will put you in jail by force. If you do not do as they say, they will meet you with violence. They certainly cannot meet you with common sense and logic. If they did, their system would crumble like a cheap cookie.

The New York Times

From Beyond the Grace Commission

Published: April 1, 1990

LEAD: To the Editor:
To the Editor:

In a recent Forum page article ("Mr. Bush, You Must Raise Taxes," Feb. 4), Representative Lee H. Hamilton, Democrat of Indiana, argued that it is impossible to cut the deficit without raising taxes. The American taxpayer should not have to bear the burden of higher taxes until waste is reduced. This is based on my experience as the chairman of the President's Private Sector Survey on Cost Control, better known as the Grace Commission. For two years, 160 of America's top business leaders probed waste, inefficiency and mismanagement in the Federal Government. Our report recommended 2,478 ways to cut wasteful Government spending without hurting the poor or disadvantaged, and without abolishing existing programs. According to the Office of Management and Budget, Grace Commission recommendations that were implemented have saved $152.4 billion.

According to the Comptroller General, Charles A. Bowsher, in a television interview, an estimated $160 *billion of income taxes paid will be wasted. In other words, the Federal Government will waste approximately 33 cents out of every $1 of individual income taxes. In spite of this blatant waste, Representative Hamilton says that we need to raise taxes because budget cuts alone are not "politically acceptable." That is not politically acceptable (to Congress) because spending is the way Congressmen get votes.*

Median-income families, whose tax bills have increased 246 times since 1948, will be the ones to carry the burden of Congressional overspending. If you asked these families, I think they would tell you that we don't need to raise taxes, we need to cut waste.

J. PETER GRACE
Chairman, W.R. Grace Inc.
New York City, Feb. 22

Source: http://query.nytimes.com/gst/fullpage.html?res=9C0CEED6143BF932A35757C0A966958260

It is impossible to ever pay the national debt with the current monetary system and exuberant government spending. When you hear politicians talking about paying down the debt, understand that it is an impossibility. Most politicians have no clue as to how money is created or how the banking world operates. They have no idea that the very money they get paid to do their jobs is created from debt. An easy way to stop the national debt is to discontinue the issuance of Federal Reserve notes and re-issue interest free United States notes. Historians and economists claim that United States notes became obsolete because Federal Reserve notes served the same needs as United States notes. Since they always omit the fact that United States notes are issued interest free, they are able to sell their story without any questions being raised. The currency that should have been put out of existence is the Federal Reserve notes. Another interesting tid-bit that they like to leave out of the debate is the fact that United States notes were bills of credit. Bills of credit are non-interest-bearing government obligations that are used as money. The first bills of credit in America were Colonial Scripts. Since the establishment of the federal government, bills of credit have been known as treasury notes or United States notes. The government issued these notes without having to accompany its issuance with interest bearing securities, such as T-notes, T-bonds and T-bills.

The Federal Reserve System was purposely designed to keep America in debt slavery. Since the inception of the Federal Reserve Act of 1913, federal government spending has steam rolled to incredible heights. In 1912, a year before the Federal Reserve Act was passed, federal spending was at about $900 million dollars. By 1917, that total had more than doubled to about $2.3 billion dollars. By the time they discontinued issuing the United States notes in 1971, federal spending was at $210 billion dollars a year. This is an incredible number even if the rate of inflation is taken into account. In the first 54 years of the Federal Reserve Systems existence, federal spending had risen over 9,000%. Since the discontinuation of the United States notes in 1971, federal spending rose another 1,300%. It is obvious that Federal Reserve notes are a detriment to the U.S. economy. This is one of many arguments for shutting down the Federal Reserve. Some believe President Kennedy was assassinated for attempting such a thing, *inter alia*.

The Misconceptions of President Kennedy's Executive Order 11110

In the June of 1963, President Kennedy signed Executive Order 11110. The order reads as follows:

Executive Order 11110

AMENDMENT OF EXECUTIVE ORDER NO. 10289 AS AMENDED, RELATING TO THE PERFORMANCE OF CERTAIN FUNCTIONS AFFECTING THE DEPARTMENT OF THE TREASURY. By virtue of the authority vested in me by section 301 of title 3 of the United States Code, it is ordered as follows:

SECTION 1. Executive Order No. 10289 of September 19, 1951, as amended, is hereby further amended - (a) By adding at the end of paragraph 1 thereof the following subparagraph (j): "(j) The authority vested in the President by paragraph (b) of section 43 of the Act of May 12, 1933, as amended (31 U.S.C. 821 (b)), to issue silver certificates against any silver bullion, silver, or standard silver dollars in the Treasury not then held for redemption of any outstanding silver certif.-icates, to prescribe the denominations of such silver certificates, <u>and to coin standard silver</u>

dollars and subsidiary silver currency for their redemption," and *(b) By revoking subparagraphs (b) and (c) of paragraph 2 thereof.*

SECTION 2. The amendment made by this Order shall not affect any act done, or any right accruing or accrued or any suit or proceeding had or commenced in any civil or criminal cause prior to the date of this Order but all such liabilities shall continue and may be enforced as if said amendments had not been made.

Federal Register page and date: 28 FR 5709; June 12, 1963

Source: http://www.archives.gov/federal-register/executive-orders/1963-kennedy.html

After Kennedy's assassination, silver certificates and silver dollars were never re-issued or re-circulated.[38] The banking elite were in the process of eliminating hard money and introducing their fiat fed notes. Another topic of interest is the removal of the redemption clause on all U.S. currencies, including Federal Reserve notes in the same year—1963.

[38] In March of 1964, Secretary of the Treasury C. Douglas Dillon halted redemption of silver certificates for silver dollars. This decision was pursuant to the act of June 4, 1963 (31 U.S.C. 405a-1). The act allowed the exchange of silver certificates for silver bullion until June 24, 1968.

John F. Kennedy was sworn in as the 35th President at noon on January 20, 1961.

Many people involved in the truth movement allege that Executive Order 11110 was intended to infuse $4.3 billion dollars of silver certificates into circulation. However, this claim is unsubstantiated. Silver certificates were discontinued in the same year of President Kennedy's executive order.[39] United States notes[40] were fiat, the same as

---

[39] Kennedy's Executive Order 11110 decision was signed on the same exact date of an Act that was passed to stop the redemption of silver certificates. *Refer to:* (31 U.S.C. 405a-1). The Act allowed the exchange of silver certificates for silver bullion until June 24, 1968. This was the deadline set by the Congress. Since that date, there has been no obligation to issue silver in any form in exchange for these certificates. According to the Treasury Department, Congress took this action because there were approximately three million silver dollars remaining in the Treasury Department's vaults. These coins had high numismatic values, and there was no way to make an equitable distribution of them among the many people holding silver certificates.

today's Federal Reserve notes. Below is a series 1963 United States note. Notice that there is no redemption clause on the face of the bill. It does not "promise to pay the bearer on demand."

United States Notes were redeemable in gold until 1933, when the United States abandoned the gold standard.

Kennedy's Executive Order 11110 is often cited as the reason why the international banking cartels were the major players in his assassination. Although I am not ready to dismiss the fact that the bankers may have seen President Kennedy as a threat, the theory claiming that it was do to the signing of Executive Order 11110 sounds and feels like a Straw Man fallacy. Here is why. The price of silver rose sharply during the 1950s. The price rose considerably above the par value of silver certificates. In 1960, it was nearing $1.29, which meant that silver dollars and certificates were worth more than a dollar. If Executive Order 11110 had issued $4.3 billion worth of silver certificates, the government would have taken a $1.2 billion dollar hit (4.3 X .29= 1.24). Hence, why hold a silver dollar when you could redeem it for actual silver and re-sell the actual silver in the market for $1.29? As the banks and big

---

[40] The 1963 series of United States notes were not backed by gold or silver.

institutions redeemed large quantities of silver certificates for bullion or silver dollars, the certificates were retired by the Treasury Department because they had lost their backing. Silver certificates could not be recirculated unless there was more silver being produced. As discussed earlier, having a currency backed by hard money[41] does not mean it cannot be manipulated by the banking cartels. Issuing more silver certificates was not going to liberate us from the international banking cartels. All they had to do was continue to dry up the silver market and we would have still been in debt slavery to them. If the order had commanded the issuance of United States notes, the Kennedy executive-order-assassination-theory would have been more plausible.

United States notes would have caused the international banking cartels more of a problem to create their debt based society. Its inherent difference to fed notes and silver certificates is the key. Remember, silver certificates[42] are payable to the bearer on demand in face value of the price set by the U.S. Congress. A United States note is paper money backed by nothing (fiat). However, it may serve to be a much better currency than fed notes because they are printed directly by the United States Treasury. Therefore, the middle man (The Federal Reserve) is not in the equation. The National Bank Act of 1863 required national banks to purchase U.S. Government securities as backing for their national bank notes. When the Federal Reserve member banks were created, they also had to adhere to the National Bank Act of 1863. However, this law does not govern the Treasury Department. If the Treasury Department issues United States notes, they would not be required to have the notes backed by anything—except

---

[41] Hard money and hard money policies are those which are opposed to fiat currency and thus in support of a specie standard, usually gold or silver.

[42] Silver certificates are still legal tender and do still circulate at their face value. Depending upon the age and condition of the certificates, however, they may have a greater value to collectors and dealers.

the full faith and trust of the United States Government. In other words, the government would not pay any interest on the notes. As a matter of fact, the Treasury Department did print interest-free United States notes in 1963. But as we have seen, this could not have been in response to Executive Order 11110.

This is a $2 United States note series 1963

President Kennedy's Executive Order 11110 makes no mention of issuing any United States notes. The executive order did not authorize the issuance of United States notes and there is no evidence to assume that Kennedy was even aware that some United States notes were being printed. There is no question that the criminal elite had President Kennedy assassinated. I am not here to defend the slave masters. I am only here to offer the best information I possibly can so that when you go before the world, you can walk upright. But, as I have stated in my previous books, I am not perfect nor do I claim to be perfect. I am only concerned with facts. I am not married to any belief system. If anything I write or say can be disproven with facts, then I will embrace and teach those facts. Play time is over. It is time to let go of any erroneous arguments. If we present this executive order argument to people who are seeking right knowledge, we are only leading them to the slaughter. I say that because when they try to repeat the erroneous argument to someone who has knowledge, they will be put in their place. Losing a debate may destroy their confidence in exposing the criminal elite. Their desire may dwindle and they may turn away from further study.

Let me show you an example of the flaw in the Kennedy executive order theory. Anyone who understands how the United States Government works would know that the executive branch of government (the president) does not have the authority to issue or regulate money. The power to coin or print money is vested in the legislative branch of government (Congress) under the authority of the United States Constitution, Article I Section VIII, which reads: *(in part)*

-To borrow money on the credit of the United States;
-To coin Money, regulate the Value thereof, and of foreign Coin, and fix the Standard of Weights and Measures
-To provide for the Punishment of counterfeiting the Securities and current Coin of the United States

If President Kennedy attempted to pass a law to print money, he would have usurped the authority of the Constitution. When Congress passes a law, it delegates that authority to enforce it. This delegation goes to the executive branch (the president). The executive branch is responsible for executing (executive) the laws of the United States. Obviously, the president does not personally execute anything. Instead, he delegates his authority to someone within his branch. The Agricultural Adjustment Act of May 12, 1933[43] was one of the laws that delegated author-

---

[43] The Agricultural Adjustment Act (Pub.L. 73-10, enacted May 12, 1933) made restrictions to farmers on the amount of crops they could produce. This law was part of President Franklin D. Roosevelt's "The New Deal" campaign to get the United States out of the Great Depression. The goal was to reduce the supply of the crops available in order to raise their value and give the agricultural market some stability. The farmers were paid subsidies by the federal government for leaving some of their fields unseeded.

ity to the president (executive branch) to issue United States notes. However, if the president were to take it upon himself to bypass the legislature and order the issuance of currency, it would be a usurpation and abuse of his authority. But of course, one can argue that presidents have routinely signed unconstitutional executive orders in the past as well as the present. My point is this. If one believes President Kennedy was going to bring the country back to the Constitution, the usurpation of the Constitution would have been a contradiction of that belief.

Kennedy's Executive Order 11110 did not create authority to issue more silver certificates. The only thing the order did was give the Secretary of the Treasury the authority to give the order to have silver certificates issued. The executive order amended a pre-existing executive order issued by President Harry Truman in 1951. President Truman signed Executive Order 10289, which states;

(*in part*)....

> "The Secretary of the Treasury is hereby designated and empowered to perform the following-described functions of the President without the approval, ratification, or other action of the President..."

***Source*: http://www.archives.gov/federal-register/codification/executive-order/10289.html**

Purchase directly and hold Treasury bills, etc., additional to present holdings.

United States is the majority stockholder, and (2) purchase directly and hold in portfolio for an agreed period or periods of time Treasury bills or other obligations of the United States Government in an aggregate sum of $3,000,000,000 in addition to those they may then hold, unless prior to the termination of such period or periods the Secretary shall consent to their sale. No suspension of reserve requirements of the Federal Reserve banks, under the terms of section 11(c) of the Federal Reserve Act, necessitated by reason of operations under this section, shall require the imposition of the graduated tax upon any deficiency in reserves as provided in said section 11(c). Nor shall it require any automatic increase in the rates of interest or discount charged by any Federal Reserve bank, as otherwise specified in that section. The Federal Reserve Board, with the approval of the Secretary of the Treasury, may require the Federal Reserve banks to take such action as may be necessary, in the judgment of the Board and of the Secretary of the Treasury, to prevent undue credit expansion.

Suspension of reserve requirements not to impose graduated tax on any deficiency in reserves.
Vol. 38, p. 262.
U.S.C., p. 276.

Interest or discount rates.

Measures to prevent undue credit expansion.

If unable to secure assent of Federal Reserve banks to authorized agreements, etc.

(b) If the Secretary, when directed by the President, is unable to secure the assent of the several Federal Reserve banks and the Federal Reserve Board to the agreements authorized in this section, or if operations under the above provisions prove to be inadequate to meet the purposes of this section, or if for any other reason additional measures are required in the judgment of the President to meet such purposes, then the President is authorized—

Authority of President.

United States notes may be issued.

Vol. 12, p. 345.

(1) To direct the Secretary of the Treasury to cause to be issued in such amount or amounts as he may from time to time order, United States notes, as provided in the Act entitled "An Act to authorize the issue of United States notes and for the redemption of funding thereof and for funding the floating debt of the United States", approved February 25, 1862, and Acts supplementary thereto and amendatory thereof, in the same size and of similar color to the Federal Reserve notes heretofore issued and in denominations of $1, $5, $10, $20, $50, $100, $500, $1,000, and $10,000; but notes issued under this subsection shall be issued only for the purpose of

Size, color, denominations, etc.

Purposes of issue defined.

The *Agricultural Adjustment Act* of May 12, 1933 (in part)

The Agricultural Adjustment Act allowed the issuance of United States notes only if the Federal Reserve failed to meet the requirement of backing their notes with United States Government securities. President Kennedy, by signing Executive Order 11110, delegated his statutory authority to issue silver certificates[44] to the Treasury of the Secretary, Clarence D. Dillon. Mr. Dillon was a big time banker, a member of the Council on Foreign Relations, as well as a close and personal friend of John D. Rockefeller III. He was also chairman of the Rockefeller Foundation from 1972 to 1975 and served alongside Rockefeller on the 1973 Commission on Private Philanthropy and Public Needs. Mr. Dillon's connection to the criminal elite should not be ignored.

To believe that Executive Order 11110 was prima facie evidence[45] that Kennedy was getting ready to issue silver certificates is a contradiction to the face of the order itself. The order expresses that Kennedy was giving the authority to issue silver certificates to Clarence Dillon, who was a banker with connections to the criminal elite. Therefore, there would be no reason to eliminate Kennedy for signing the order because it was giving the bankers the power they coveted. President Kennedy, perhaps unknowingly, handed the power to issue hard money over to the bankers.

---

[44] Remember, silver certificates were actually warehouse receipts for certain amounts of silver that were with the Treasury of the United States. However, United States notes are government issued certificates, or bills of credit. They are redeemable in payment of government taxes and other dues which are due to the United States Government.

[45] *Prima facie* is a Latin expression meaning "on its first appearance", or "by first instance". Prima facie evidence is defined as; Evidence that is sufficient to raise a presumption of fact or to establish the fact in question, unless the evidence has been rebutted.

The New York Times

By ERIC PACE
Published: January 12, 2003

C. Douglas Dillon, a versatile Wall Street financier who was named secretary of the Treasury by President Kennedy and ambassador to France under President Eisenhower, and was a longtime executive of the Metropolitan Museum of Art, died Friday at New York Presbyterian Hospital in Manhattan. Mr. Dillon, who lived with his wife on Jupiter Island in Hobe Sound, Fla., was 93.

Mr. Dillon was born to wealth and influence as the son of the founder of Dillon, Read & Company, an international banking house. Mr. Dillon was widely respected for his attention to detail -- he had a reputation for ferreting out inconspicuous errors in reports -- and his intellect, which his parents began shaping at an early age by enrolling Mr. Dillon in elite private schools.

Mr. Dillon is said to have been able to read quickly and to fully comprehend what he read by the time he was 4 years old. At the Pine Lodge School in Lakehurst, N.J., Mr. Dillon's schoolmates included Nelson, Laurance and John Rockefeller III. Mr. Dillon later graduated magna cum laude from

Harvard and sharpened his analytical powers on Wall Street.

Strapping and strong-jawed, Mr. Dillon sometimes seemed self-effacing or even shy in public, despite his long prominence in public affairs and in business. He served over the years as chairman of the Rockefeller Foundation, president of Harvard University's board of overseers, chairman of the Brookings Institution, vice chairman of the Council on Foreign Relations, and, after his time in Paris, in high posts at the State Department.

Refer to:
http://query.nytimes.com/gst/fullpage.html?res=9A0CE5DB1731F931A25752C0A9659C8B63

Do you see how this argument of Executive Order 11110 is fatally flawed? This order did not have anything to do with the Kennedy assassination. There is no question that President Kennedy was eliminated by several key elements of the criminal elite. However, it was not because he delegated the authority to print silver certificates to his Secretary Treasurer. No silver certificates or silver dollars were printed in 1963. The big bankers had already moved from hard money to soft money.

There are pros and cons to both soft money and hard money. As stated earlier, the best system is one in which the amount of money in circulation equals the amount of goods and services in the economy. This will allow the market to dictate the value of the currency. It appears that the bankers have settled on a fiat monetary system. The current fiat monetary system is probably the easiest in which to create a debt based economy. If one studies history, they will learn that a debt-based economy has been the direction all along. This is why they have passed a plethora of laws since the inception of the Federal Reserve System. For instance, the Coinage Act of *1965*, Pub.L. 89-81, 79 Stat. 254, enacted July 23, 1965, eliminated silver from circulating in dimes and quarter dollars. The act also diminished the silver content of the half dollar from 90% to 40%. This act was in response to coin shortages caused by the rising price of silver. The price was no doubt manipulated by the over aggressive buying of the international banking cartels.[46] This is the same old strategy. They create or manipulate the crisis and then offer the solution. After our current economic collapse, we should expect a double dose of socialistic programs and unconstitutional laws that are designed to maintain the sheep (we the people).

[46] The international banking cartels include the central banks of the advanced industrialized nations with the Bank of England leading the way. It also includes big banks like Citibank, Bank of America, and the big brokerage houses—such as JP Morgan and Goldman Sachs.

THE FRAUD OF MONEY AND BANKING

CHAPTER V.

THE CREDIT CARD RACKET

Credit card debt is running rampant in nearly all industrialized nations. In the United States alone, there are an estimated 640 million credit cards. That is an astronomical number for a population of only 290 million people. Those numbers suggest about two credit cards per person. The tragedy of it all is that there is no positive or good that comes from using credit cards. According to the American Bankers' Association, the average family carries about $2,200 in credit card debt. According to CardWeb.com, a service that tracks credit card trends, the average debt per American household with at least one credit card was $8,940 in 2002.[47] Most people tend to spend more when they use credit cards instead of actual cash. When people use credit cards, there is no emotional attachment to their hard earned money. They tend to just flip that plastic out and swipe it. A couple of extra dollars for an item does not seem to matter. It is a big difference from cashing your

[47] The $8,940 is inclusive of any other debt. According to the ABA, about $2,200 of that total was due to credit cards.

paycheck and going out to buy goods and services. When we are taking money out of our wallet or purse, we could feel the hours we worked to get that money. This is not the case with credit cards. There is no emotional attachment because you have made your purchase and you still have the same amount of cash in your pocket.

Since credit cards do not fall under M1, M2 or M3, they are not considered to be part of the money supply. However, credit cards have helped erode the economy. Instead of depositing money in a savings account or purchasing goods and services to help the economy flow, many people are using a good chunk of their hard earned money to basically pay the interest rates on their credit card bills. We are talking about over a whopping 20% interest. In some cases, credit cards are charging 27% interest. There was a time when your local district attorney could charge these companies with the felony of criminal usury. Do you see how that works? All they had to do was create a law that allows them to do as they please. Now, I believe in a free market and the theory of a *laissez faire*[48] economic system. However, credit card companies have always suckered people in with low introductory interest rates. This is insidious, for the reason that credit card companies offer their cards to unsuspecting people who believe they are getting a bargain on the interest rate. After charging a couple of thousand dollars on the card, the interest rate begins to move north of the introductory rate. But here is the kicker. If you happen to have charged $3,000 on the card at the introductory low rate, when they pump your interest rate up to over 20%, the new rate applies to the outstanding balance on your account. Hence, it is as if you started with the inflated rate anyway. If the rate changes, they are not going to apply the change to only the new charges while keeping the lower interest

---

[48] Laissez faire is the theory or system of government that upholds the autonomous character of the economic order, believing that government should intervene as little as possible in the direction of economic affairs.

rate on the old charges. They apply the new ballooned interest rate across the board.

USA TODAY

Why banks are boosting credit card interest rates and fees

Updated 11/14/2008 3:00 PM

By Kathy Chu and Byron Acohido, USA TODAY

Tommy Newsom was shocked when his bank nearly doubled his credit card interest rate this year, to 27%, for no apparent reason. A customer rep told him the law allowed the bank to do so, and that was all the justification it needed. "I never missed a payment," says Newsom, 63, of Mesquite, Texas, who owes about $5,000 on the card. "The bank is just looking for a reason to maximize profits." In recent years, banks have sharply raised interest rates and penalty fees on credit cards. As the economy tanks and banks' mortgage-related losses balloon, some banks are stepping up such increases to boost revenue. Bearing the brunt are consumers for whom a jump in rates and fees can make it tougher to pay their bills at a time when household budgets already are being stretched.

A key driver behind this trend: securitization. From 2003 to 2007, seven of the largest issuers of credit cards packaged an increasing amount of card debt into securities and sold them to investors, just as banks did with mortgages, a USA TODAY review of banking records found. Selling off credit card debt has given banks a powerful incentive to raise card fees and penalties, according to interviews with dozens of industry analysts, academics and investment specialists. Here's why: When banks package and sell card debt, they pass along to investors some of the risk the debt will go bad. Yet, banks often get to pocket much of the profit from rate and fee increases on those accounts. Imposing higher fees on more accounts — without a comparable rise in risk — lets banks raise revenue and keep profits up, at customers' expense. Securitization has been a "major impetus" for banks to expand penalty fees and rates in recent years, says Adam Levitin, a Georgetown University law professor and card expert. Banks "have little to lose if they squeeze too hard (if consumers default), but a lot to gain if they can extract additional payments" from card users, he says.

Read the complete article at:
http://www.usatoday.com/money/industries/banking/2008-11-09-bank-credit-card-interest-rates_N.htm

Credit Cards- A brief history

Although the use of the credit card was perfected in the 1960s, the idea was born out of an 1887 novel written by Edward Bellamy entitled, *Looking Backward.* In the book, *Looking Backward*, an upper-class man from 1887 awakens in the year 2000 from a hypnotic trance to find himself in a socialist utopia. Edward Bellamy and his cousin, Francis Bellamy (the creator of the pledge of allegiance), were known to be socialists. It is important to understand that one of the main reasons why the people of the United States have succumbed to socialism is because they were suckered into debt. If someone is starving, they will accept anything. After the Great Depression of the 1930s, the people were ready to bow down to the international bankers. This allowed President Franklin D. Roosevelt to look like a hero—while at the same time introducing the American people to his administrations socialistic policies of the *New Deal.*[49]

According to some encyclopedias, such as the Britannica, the concept of credit cards originated in the United States during the roaring 1920s. The cards were not made from plastic the way they are today. Some were not even cards. Some companies issued their credit on tokens made from metal coins, metal plates, fiber, and paper cardboard. In 1938, some companies began to experiment with accepting each others credit cards.

The first bank recognized for issuing a credit card was the Flatbush National Bank of Brooklyn in New York. An employee named John Biggins invented the *Charge-It Program* between bank customers and local companies. Because there were no computers during this period, merchants would deposit sales slips in the bank. This enabled

---

[49] The *New Deal* was a list of programs initiated by the Roosevelt administration during the Great Depression.

payment by the bank. The bank would then bill the customers who used the credit.

The modern day credit card is a mutation of the charge card. Many people use these terms interchangeably. However, there are differences between a charge card and a credit card. A credit card usually allows for a minimum balance to be paid, as oppose to a charge card, which has a balance due every month or every set period as provided by the terms of the charge agreement.

The first truly independent credit card on the planet was the Diners Club card of 1950. It was founded by Frank McNamara, Casey Taylor and Ralph Schneider. The idea was to create a charge card that could be accepted by different merchants. Before the creation of the Diners Club card, many individual companies were in the practice of extending credit to their customers by setting up charge accounts. In those days, credit cards only involved sales between the merchant offering the credit and the customer. Originally, a Diners Club card was only used to pay restaurant bills. The intent was to give the dining member a feeling of security. The theory was that the person(s) dining did not have to carry a great deal of cash when going out to eat in restaurants.

In 1966, the Bank of America created the "Bank-America Service Corporation." This creation would later be re-named VISA.[50] Also taking place in 1966, a group of credit-issuing banks joined together and founded the Inter-Bank Card Association. This association is now known as MasterCard. A top bank in the United Kingdom also set up shop in 1966. Barclaycard was the first to launch a credit card outside of the United States. Barclaycard is currently one of Europe's leading issuers of credit cards.

---

[50] The name "VISA" was not publicly recognized until 1976.

The Creation of Credit Card Debt

As the number of people with credit cards began to increase in the 1970s and early 1980s, the federal funds rate nearly rose to a 20% charge. The rise was due to the excessive tightening of the money supply by the Federal Open Market Committee (FOMC).[51] It was costing credit card banks 20% interest to borrow money, and they were only earning 10% to 14% interest on their credit card accounts. This was before the landmark Supreme Court case of *Marquette Nat. Bank of Minneapolis v. First of Omaha Service Corp.* Prior to this ruling, all interest rates were regulated by the state in which the card holder was located. The *Marquette* decision changed the law by ruling that state anti-usury laws regulating interest rates cannot be enforced against nationally-chartered banks based in other states. Therefore, if your credit card company is chartered in South Dakota, which allows a bank to charge 25% interest, but you live in New York, which allows less than 10% interest, the New York card holder would have to pay the 25% rate of (South Dakota) where the bank is located.

Before the *Marquette* decision, credit card companies were losing money. The cost of borrowing money became greater than the interest rates they were allowed to charge. South Dakota was the first state to change their usury laws and increase the amount of lawful interest rates a lender could offer a customer. This caused Citibank to create a charter for their credit card division in South Dakota. Soon thereafter, other states and large nationally

---

[51] By trading government securities, the Fed affects the federal funds rate, which is the interest rate at which depository institutions lend money to each other overnight. The Federal Open Market Committee establishes the target rate for trading in the federal funds market.

chartered banks followed the example. This was a victory for the banks and a loss for the people.

In the landmark case of *Smiley v. Citibank (South Dakota),* the Supreme Court of the United States again held that the National Bank Act of 1864 authorizes a credit card company to charge the interest rate of the state in which it is chartered (located). The court also rejected the arguments that late payment fees do not constitute interest.

Today, credit card companies are allowed to charge interest rates that a generation ago would have been the domain of the loan sharks. The fraudsters at the top of this scam have pumped a lot of misinformation and mythology into the financial world. Even intelligent people in the financial industry will claim debt is a tool to create prosperity and economic growth. They forget to mention that with the prosperity (usually short lived) come the bust and the depressions. The truth of the matter is that the debt society which has been put above our heads is designed to keep us struggling without any relief. Most people are never going to get out of debt unless they hit the lottery or find a fortune lying around somewhere. In one lifetime, debt brings enough risk to offset any advantage that could be gained by taking on that debt.

The numbers given by the American Bankers Association paint a rosy picture when it comes to how much credit card debt the people are in. I gave you their conservative number of $2,200 credit card debt per family with the understanding that statistics can be manipulated. For example, if you have four people in a room with an average age of 48, you may think that you might be able to hang out with them if you are 47 or 48 years of age. However, the four people can easily be 25, 10, 75, and 85 years old. You may have the average in common, but you do not have the age in common. This is what statistics tend to do. It only polls a certain amount of people. It surveys them and then averages out the answers to include people the statistics did not survey.

We all know that people lie about money all the time. If you asked a friend or family member about their credit card debt, you probably would not get a straight answer. That is the sad truth about credit cards. Most people are in credit card debt but no one wants to talk about it. What makes things worse is the fact that credit card companies are selling your debt to bottom feeding debt collectors. In most cases, credit card accounts are sold for pennies on the dollar. This takes place even if the credit card company received insurance for the underperforming account. In the case of the latter, only the insurance company can sue for damages as a subrogee.[52]

Here is what is usually taking place after your credit card is charged off[53] by the credit card company.

1. *The credit card company has their money as a result of having the account insured.*
2. *The debt collector spent pennies on the dollar to acquire your account and you are the one who is having his/her bank account or paycheck ravaged by these fraudsters.*

Credit card billing statements cannot be sold for value because the use of credit cards are a series of continuing offers to contract. These are not negotiable instruments. However, credit card companies continue to treat these billing statements as a negotiable instrument. This is a fraud! A signed credit card application is not a contract or any type of promissory note!!

---

[52] A subrogee is the person or entity that assumes the legal right to attempt to collect a claim of another (subrogor) in return for paying the other's expenses or debts which the other claims against a third party. A subrogee is usually the insurance company which has insured the party whose expenses were paid. Thus, the subrogee insurance company may file a lawsuit against a party which caused the damages to its insured which the subrogee paid.

[53] An account is charged off when the creditor deems it to be an uncollectible debt, or "bad debt". Generally, this is when six months has passed since the date of the first missed payment.

There are hundreds of thousands, if not millions, of people being cheated by debt collectors, lawyers, and judges in this whole debt collection racket. Debt collectors are buying these credit card debts and suing people without any legal precedence. Judges are handing out judgments that are void, no good, and unenforceable.[54] In the New Jersey credit card case of *Novack v. Cities Service Oil Co.*, the courts ruled as such:

The conclusion that the issuance of a credit card does not create a contract includes an analysis of the concept of consideration. It is well settled that to be enforceable a contract must be supported by valuable consideration. Coast National Bank v. Bloom , 113 N.J.L. 597 (E. & A. 1934); Fryns v. Fair Lawn Fur Dressing Co. , 114 N.J. Eq. 462 (Ch. 1933); Levine v. Blumenthal , 117 N.J.L. 426 (Sup. Ct. 1936). Consideration involves a detriment incurred by the promisee or a benefit received by the promisor, at the promisor's request. *In the credit card relationship, neither status is created. The holder of the card (promisee) is free to cancel or not use it, and has gratuitously received an opportunity to purchase without incurring any detriment. Additionally, there does not appear to be any benefit bargained for or received by the issuing company (promisor). Lacking consideration, the credit card account is, as stated in City Stores Co. v. Henderson , 116 Ga. App. 114, 156 S.E. 2 d 818 (App. Ct. 1967), a continuing offer to purchase which may be withdrawn by either party at any time.*

Basically, however, a credit card is nothing more than an indication to sellers of commodities that the person who has received a credit card from the issuer thereof has a satisfactory credit rating and that if credit is extended, the issuer of the credit card will pay (or see to it that the seller of the commodity receives payment) for the merchandise delivered. See, Lit Brothers v. Haines , 98 N.J.L. 658, 121 A. 131 (Sup. Ct. 1923); Jordan v. J. C. Penney , 114 Ga. App. 822, 152 S.E. 2 d 786 (App. Ct. 1966); see generally; 46 A.L.R. 3 d 1383.

***Novack v. Cities Service Oil Co.*, 374 A.2d 89, 149 N.J.Super. 549 (N.J.Super.Law Div. 04/07/1977)**

Do you see that? Credit card debt does not create a negotiable instrument. A separate contract is created every time you use the credit card. What the credit card companies are doing is selling account statements to debt collectors. This is not enforceable under any theory of a

---

[54] For the most part, the judges involved in this fraud are from the lower courts, i.e. municipal and county courts.

holder-in-due-course.[55] In nearly all cases, they are selling charged-off accounts. When an account is charged-off the creditor writes off the account balance as a bad debt. It usually occurs after the account has been in default for six months or 60 days after receiving notification of bankruptcy from the court. A charge-off basically means that they no longer count your debt on their books as an asset. This is done in accordance with the principals set by the Generally Accepted Accounting Principles [56]*(GAAP)* and the FFIEC[57] (Federal Financial Institutions Examination Council). A charge-off does not mean, however, that you do not owe the debt. They would still have a right to collect the debt up until the statute of limitations expires. Statutes of limitations are laws that set the deadline or maximum period of time within which a lawsuit or claim may be filed. After such time, the creditor may still attempt to collect the debt. However, they may not use the courts to enforce payment of that debt.

Some debt collectors purchase evidence of debt that is years beyond the statute of limitations. Because they purchase these accounts for pennies on the dollar, in some cases, they will make a profit even if they are able to recover only $10. They typically violate the Fair Debt Col-

---

[55] According to the Uniform Commercial Code found at § 3-302, a holder-in-due course is a party who becomes the good faith holder of a negotiable instrument (such as a check, note, or draft), for value received, without knowledge of any claims or defaults against it.

[56] Generally Accepted Accounting Principles, also known as GAAP, are a combination of authoritative standards (set by policy boards) and simply the commonly accepted ways of recording and reporting accounting information.

[57] The FFIEC is a formal interagency body empowered to prescribe uniform principles, standards, and report forms for the federal examination of financial institutions by the Board of Governors of the Federal Reserve System (FRB), the Federal Deposit Insurance Corporation (FDIC), the National Credit Union Administration (NCUA), the Office of the Comptroller of the Currency (OCC), and the Office of Thrift Supervision (OTS), and to make recommendations to promote uniformity in the supervision of financial institutions.

lections Practices Act by falsely alleging that the statute of limitations starts from the time the debt collector purchased the account.

The current economy has debt collectors in the type of heaven that they could only dream of. Many Americans are in arrears[58] on credit card bills, mortgage payments, and are defaulting on student and auto loans. The criminal elite made sure that you would have no relief. A 2005 bankruptcy law rewrite has made it difficult for consumers to file for protection from creditors.

Selling bad credit card debt and many other debts has become big business in the debt collection racket. The amount of bad credit card debts sold to debt collectors has more than doubled since the year 2000. These numbers are staggering—from $27 billion in the year 2000, to more than $59 billion in 2006.

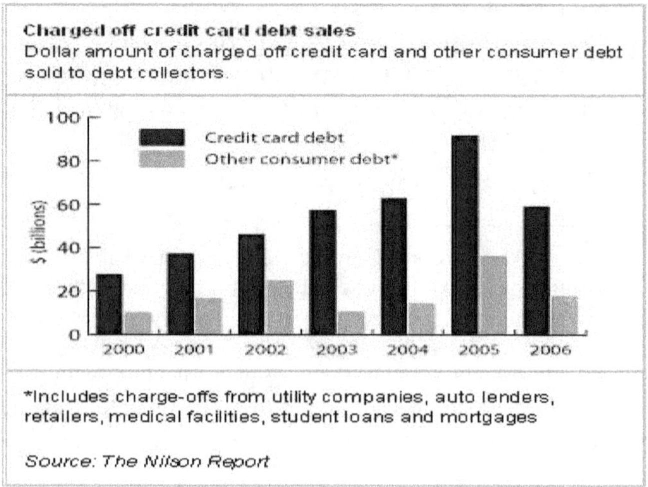

[58] The state of being behind or late, esp. in the fulfillment of a duty, promise, obligation, or the like. Also something overdue in payment; a debt that remains unpaid.

Getting out of Credit Card debt

There is no easy way to get out of debt. The best advice is to not incur any more debt. Nevertheless, if you manage to get out of debt, do not ever get back in. Many people get out of debt and then get sucked right back in. It is important to understand that the criminal elite want you to be in debt. The first step to becoming free and independent would be to free oneself from debt. But, even so, try to avoid using debt relief companies that sell you "get out of debt quick" schemes. There is no such thing as getting out of debt instantly—unless you have the money to do so. Most schemes that promise to get you out of debt in an instant are usually fraudulent and very costly. For the price of this written documentary, you will have important weapons at your disposal to make a good attempt at getting out of credit card debt. Let us go step by step.

Suggestion 1: Make it a fundamental part of the way you shop and spend that if you cannot pay for something with available funds, you cannot afford it. Stop taking on new debt. If you really aspire to get out of the hole you are in, stop digging. When the digging has stopped, then you can worry about getting out. Do not be fooled into believing that there is a such thing as good debt.

Suggestion 2: Pay credit cards off from the largest interest rate to the smallest. Make the minimum payments on all your credit cards except the one with the largest interest rate. Pay as much as you possibly can on the one with the highest interest rate. This method differs from that of many professionals such as Dave Ramsey,[59] who suggest pay-

[59] Dave Ramsey is a well respected financial expert and the author of *The Total Money Makeover*: A proven plan for financial fitness. Published by Thomas Nelson Pub., 2003 ISBN 0785263268.

ing off debts from the smallest to the largest regardless of interest rate. The wisdom behind that strategy is the psychological advantage of clearing one or two credit cards ASAP.[60] I am not interested in psychology as much as I am in getting out of the hole as soon as possible. However, I suggest for you to do which ever makes you more comfortable. My point is to immediately do something! Once you get yourself out of debt, make it your business to stay out. Say goodbye to credit cards forever.

Once you are free from credit card debt, you will have no more sleepless nights over how to bring down mounting credit card balances. Do not buy into the popular notion of getting a credit card to use for emergency purposes. Once you are out of credit card debt, you will be able to save enough money to create the cushion needed to absorb most emergencies. And, since you will not be in debt after resolving the emergency (as you would if paid with a credit card), you will be in a much better financial position. If you could only save $50 a week, you will accumulate $2,600 in one year. If you can save $100 a week, it will result in $5,200 a year.[61] Consider these amounts the equivalent to the credit line of any emergency credit card. Now, if a year goes by without any emergencies, open another savings account and put half of what you saved in that account. You should use one account as the main savings account, and you should use the other as the emergency account. Always use the main savings account to fund a checking account for paying bills. Once you have this system established, half of the emergency account should be transferred over to the main savings account once every year. If you have the discipline to do this for 2 or 3 years, there is no reason why you cannot accumulate a cushion of at least $7,000.

---

[60] An Idiom (acronym) meaning; As Soon As Possible. It is pronounced letter by letter, or as a single word, /āsap/. Also written as A.S.A.P

[61] The goal is to save as much as you can. If you could only afford to save $25 a week, then do so. But, if you can save $200, then it is recommended that you do so.

THE FRAUD OF MONEY AND BANKING

CHAPTER VI.

THE GREAT COLLAPSE

As the first decade of the twenty-first century comes to an end in two and a half years, the U.S. dollar will not lead the economies of the world into the next decade. The U.S. economy is in freefall. Layoffs are soaring, home building is plunging, and stocks are falling off a cliff. The preaching of a strong dollar policy by the Bush administration and the Fed Chairman, Ben Bernanke, were nothing more than political talking points. Continued massive trade deficits and a whopping national debt have put the U.S. dollar in a very precarious position. The same people that propped up the U.S. dollar are the very same people bringing it down.

The U.S. dollar is slowly, but surely, losing its status as the world's reserve currency. This is something the United States has enjoyed since the aftermath of World War II. In September of 2008, Chinese banks were told to put the brakes on lending to U.S. banks. The Chinese have over $1 trillion dollars in assets. If they sold these assets, it would result in the further devaluation of the dollar and it will cause bond yield rates to rise. As the dollar continues to plunge, the United States Government would have to offer higher interest on their securities to entice investors to purchase them. That translates into more debt for the people.

The current financial meltdown is shaping up to be the worst economic collapse in world history. Do not be fooled into believing that the criminals responsible for this collapse are working toward a solution that will benefit you. The implementation of the bailout bills are in contradiction to a solution. The Bush and Obama bailout bills are intended to further the collapse. Let me explain how traverse these so-called bailouts have been since the beginning. The financial institutions (who have and will receive funds from the bailout bill) trade and do their dealings in dollar denominated instruments. They also hold a substantial chunk of government debt securities, such as Treasury bills, Treasury bonds, and Treasury notes. In a crazy way, this makes these financial institutions creditors of the United States Government. To finance the bailout, the government must eventually borrow some of the money back from these same institutions. As you already know, the borrowing occurs when the banks purchase government securities. And, to add to this fraud, the government will then pay the bankers interest on the securities the bankers would purchase with the bailout money. Do you see why the bailout banker bill could not be, and is not, designed to fix anything? Ladies and gentlemen of the jury, the American people have been hornswoggled[62] once again.

The government and the bankers are financing their indebtness at the expense of the American taxpayer. They have laid down a yellow brick road that leads to the consolidation and centralization of power in the financial industry. All of these tactics are being put in place to collapse the U.S. dollar.

---

[62] To cheat somebody: to trick or deceive somebody through misleading statements or falsehoods. Also to perplex somebody: to make somebody confused.

The Dollar Peg

Many economists and professionals in the financial world are making attempts to figure out why the economy is tanking. They do not suspect that this financial crisis was purposely engineered. These demons (criminal elite) know exactly what they are doing. The former Fed-Chairman Alan Greenspan told the oil producing Arab countries to drop the dollar peg. Pegging is a method of fixing a country's currency to stay at a certain rate below or above another country's currency. After World War II, the United States became the number one financial super power of the world. Most industrialized countries began pegging their currency to the U.S. dollar. When a country pegs their money to a commodity such as gold, silver, or uranium, the value of the currency would then be in direct proportion to the value of the commodity. In order to maintain the local exchange rate, the central bank buys and sells its own currency on the foreign exchange market in return for the currency to which it is pegged. The central bank of the foreign country pegged to the dollar will have to ensure that it can supply the market with those dollars. In order to maintain the rate, the foreign central bank must keep a high level of dollar reserves. This reserved amount of dollars held by the foreign central bank is used to release (or absorb) extra funds into (or out of) the market. This ensures an appropriate money supply, appropriate fluctuations in the market (inflation/deflation), and ultimately, the exchange rate. All exchange rates are "floating" in reality. Some are fixed only in theory. In theory because central banks always adjust the official exchange rate when necessary.

A floating exchange rate is determined by the private market through supply and demand. A floating rate is usually referred to as self-correcting because any differences in supply and demand will automatically be corrected in the market.

This formula is very simple. If foreign countries lose faith in the dollar, they will sell their dollar reserves. What happens to the value of something that is being sold without any demand for it? It depreciates in value. This is what is happening to the U.S. dollar. Do you believe the former Federal Reserve Board Chairman, Alan Greenspan, does not know this principal? Of course he does! Why then, would he tell foreigners to drop the dollar?

REUTERS

Drop dollar peg, ex-Fed chair tells Arabs

Reuters

Published: Tuesday, February 26, 2008

Former Federal Reserve chairman Alan Greenspan said on Monday near-record Gulf Arab inflation would fall "significantly" if oil producers dropped their dollar pegs, in contradiction to Saudi policy.

The pegs restrict the Gulf's ability to fight inflation by forcing them to shadow U.S. monetary policy at a time when the Fed is cutting rates to ward off recession and gulf economies are surging on a near fivefold jump in oil prices since 2002.

Rifts are growing across the world's top oil-exporting region on how to tackle inflation which hit a 27-year peak of seven per cent in Saudi Arabia in January and a 19-year peak of 9.3 per cent in the United Arab Emirates in 2006, the most recent figure.

"In the short term, free floating . . . will not fully dissipate inflationary pressure, although it would significantly do so," Greenspan told an investment conference in Jeddah, Saudi Arabia's second-largest city. Saudi and UAE central bank chiefs spoke in favour on Monday of retaining dollar pegs, while Qatar's prime minister advocated regional currency reform to avert possible unilateral revaluations designed to curb inflation.

"The economies of the Gulf and the United States are completely out of sync and that is exposing the shortcomings of the dollar peg," said Simon Williams, Middle East economist at HSBC Holdings Plc in Dubai.

Alan Greenspan is not a dummy. These people know exactly what they are doing. In 2002 Greenspan was awarded the honorary title of *Knight Commander of the British Empire*. He has also been bestowed commander of the *Légion d'honneur* (Legion of Honor). The highest of these orders is that of the *Grand Cross*. The order of the *Grand Cross* is traced back to the original modern day bankers, the Knights Templar. One has to wonder if Alan Greenspan's loyalty is to the United States, or the Crowns of England and France. Below is the star of the *Knights Grand Cross Order of The British Empire*. Notice what it reads; "FOR GOD AND THE EMPIRE."

Which God and which empire are people like Alan Greenspan loyal to?

The Emergency Economic Stabilization Act of 2008

Some Americans are still under the impression that the banker bailout bill was to help mortgage companies and people who are struggling to pay their mortgages. The mortgages are supposed to be helped under the TARP (Troubled Assets Relief Program) provision of the Bush bailout bill. The Office of Financial Stability is a new office within the Office of Domestic Finance of the United States Treasury created by the Emergency Economic Stabilization Act of 2008 to operate TARP. On October 6, 2008, merely days after the bailout bill was officially passed, it was announced that Neel Kashkari, a former executive at Goldman Sachs, would be the interim head of the Office of Financial Stability. Kashkari joined the Treasury Department in July of 2006 as a Senior Advisor to U.S. Treasury Secretary Henry Paulson—who is also a former Goldman Sachs Executive. Kashkari worked for a defense contracting company named *Northrop Grumman Space Technology*[63] up until June of 2000. While at Grumman, he worked as a design engineer in the Mechanical Engineering Department. How does someone make such a drastic change in careers? Kashkari went from being an engineer for a defense contractor to working on Wall Street? Something does not smell right. I bet it is the relationship between the War on Terror, and the financial institutions. The financial institutions are making billions of dollars from the War on Terror.

The bankers are now creating the necessary conditions to give themselves the rest of the regulatory powers

[63] Northrop Grumman was formally known as TRW.

they only appear to lack. The management of the money resources of the United States has always been the primary function of the Treasury Department. However, the Treasury Department has been hijacked by the bankers.

On September 2, 1789, Congress approved an act to establish the Treasury Department of the United States. Some of the duties imposed on the Treasury Department are as follows:

(in part).....

> **Section 5.** ***And be it further enacted***, That it shall be the duty of the Auditor to receive all public accounts, and after examination to certify the balance, and transmit the accounts with the vouchers and certificate to the Comptroller for his decision thereon: ***Provided***, That if any person whose account shall be so audited, be dissatisfied therewith, he may within six months appeal to the Comptroller against such settlement.
>
> **Section 6.** ***And be it further enacted***, That is shall be the duty of the Register to keep all accounts of the receipts and expenditures of the public money, and of all debts due to or from the United States; to receive from the Comptroller the accounts which shall have been finally adjusted, and to preserve such accounts with their vouchers and certificates; to record all warrants for the receipt or payment of monies at the Treasury, certify the same thereon, and to transmit to the Secretary of the Treasury, copies of the certificates of balances of accounts adjusted as is herein directed.

Basically, the bankers already have the authority granted to the Treasury Department. The bankers have taken this authority by stealth.[64] Now they want it by law and as a matter of fact.

The infamous bailout bill (Emergency Economic Stabilization Act of 2008) passed by the Bush administration was only the beginning of the end for the current monetary system. If you thought the old system was corrupt, wait until you get a load of the one they are forming. This $700 billion bailout bill was designed by the bank lobbyists themselves. This fraud is right in front of our face. However, the $700 billion dollar bailout is a smoke screen. The real issue is the fact that the bankers want to privatize the U.S. Treasury Department and give themselves immunity from any wrong doing. While we kept hearing about the $700 billion, the Federal Reserve was busy injecting $900 billion in liquidity to the banks. Think about this. If they can lend or give the banks money (our money), what is the need for new legislature (laws) to enact what they are and have already been doing? The answer is simple. It is not about a $700 billion dollar bailout. It is about taking the current monetary order into a new era; the new age, the new way of controlling and maintaining the slaves. When you peel back all the crap, you will see that this is what the 2008 banker bailout was primarily about. It has nothing to do with helping the economy or the troubled housing market. *Refer to appendix C*

The American economy must implode in order for the criminal elite to introduce you to the North American Union and the amero. The same thing is happening in the oil producing Gulf States. You also have the African Union coming into form. All of these unions translate into more power in fewer hands. The world will be ever so close to a one world state.

---

[64] Merriam Webster's dictionary defines the word stealth as: 1 a*archaic* something stolen2**:** the act or action of proceeding furtively, secretly, or imperceptibly <the state moves by *stealth* to gather information — Nat Hentoff>3**:** the state of being furtive or unobtrusive. It also defines "furtive" as; obtained underhandedly.

CNNMoney.com
A Service of CNN, Fortune & Money

Fed pumps billions more into banks

Central bank doubles to $300 billion the amount it will loan banks. Loans could reach $900 billion by end of year.

By Chris Isidore, CNNMoney.com senior writer
Last Updated: October 7, 2008: 10:25 AM ET

NEW YORK (CNNMoney.com) -- The Federal Reserve announced Monday that it will increase by hundreds of billions of dollars the money it makes available to the nation's banks.

The central bank said that its so-called term auction facility, which accepts financial instruments such as mortgage-backed securities as collateral, will be doubled immediately to $300 billion. The total amount available to banks will rise to $600 billion under the moves announced Monday.

In addition, the Fed signaled it could increase the amount available through those loans to $900 billion by the end of the year, increasing the amount the Fed will loan through the program by $750 billion above its previous limit.

The moves come in the wake of the passage on Friday of a $700 billion bailout bill that will allow Treasury to buy damaged assets directly from banks and Wall Street firms.

Experts said the moves by the Fed were an acknowledgement that many of the nation's leading financial institutions may not be able to wait until Treasury sets up its program. It may take weeks or perhaps even months before the Treasury can pump billions into the system itself by buying the damaged assets held on their balance sheets.

"The crisis in credit markets has become very acute, not just here but in Europe as well," said Lyle Gramley, a former Fed governor who is now an economist with the Stanford Group. "In a situation like this, you have to provide all the liquidity that is needed so that illiquid institutions don't become insolvent institutions." The rapid expansion of the Fed program is essentially like an emergency bridge loan for institutions caught in a credit squeeze, said Kevin Giddis, head of fixed-income sales trading and research for investment firm Morgan Keegan.

The Fed had little choice but to try to pump as much cash as possible into the system, no matter the risks associated with taking damaged assets as collateral, Giddis said. "Liquidity is needed immediately, and we're talking hours," he said. "I think the Fed will continue to take whatever steps it can until we unlock the problem." Giddis and Gramley both agree that the Fed appears to be focused on these kinds of non-traditional measures to pump cash into the market rather than simply cutting interest rates, which is how the central bank has historically spurred a slowing economy. But neither would rule out the possibility that the Fed will do an emergency rate cut before its Oct. 28 and 29 meeting if problems in credit markets continue to worsen.

Read the entire article at:
http://money.cnn.com/2008/10/06/news/economy/fed_loans/

The taxpayer will feel the brunt of the downside risk of pumping all this liquidity into the economy. But nevertheless, the taxpayer will not participate in any potential upside. The plan does not include giving the taxpayer anything except higher taxes and a higher rate of inflation. It was nearly comical when they told us that the bailout was to help our economy. Whose economy were they talking about? It must have been the economy of their pockets!

The recipients of this bailout played key roles in collapsing our economy. Now many people believe that Lord Obama is going to save them from the big bad bankers. Do we understand that Obama voted for the bailout? And why wouldn't he? The bankers put their money Behind his campaign. It is insane to believe that Obama will stop what the bankers have started. This collapse is artificial (as they all are). Let us examine. They have created the subprime mortgage crisis, the credit crunch (do to the outrageous interest rates on credit cards)[65] and the continued devaluation of the dollar *inter-alia*. Now we have Obama spewing rhetoric about how he is going to make sure the banks are held accountable. Meanwhile, he is filling his cabinet with bankers, members of the Council on Foreign Relations, and former Clinton and daddy Bush cabinet members. This was foretold in Volume One: *The Conspiracy Theory Fraud*. All Obama has done is appointed people who have caused the United States to get into the mess that it is in today. Obama's candidates for treasury top dog were:

Lawrence Summers: played a key role in lobbying Congress for the repeal of the Glass-Steagall Act. In 1999, as Treasury Secretary, he spearheaded the adoption of the Financial Services Modernization Act. From 1991 till 1993, he served as Chief Economist for the World Bank. While at the World Bank, he signed a memo written by a member of his staff proposing that free trade would not necessarily benefit the

---

[65] Credit Card rates are never influence by the fed funds rate or the prime rate. It is solely based on the discretion of the credit card company.

environment in developing countries. An aside to the memo, leaked to the press, said that "The economic logic behind dumping a load of toxic waste in the lowest wage country is impeccable and we should face up to that." The leaked memo was the subject of public controversy.

Paul Volker was chairman of the Federal Reserve Board in the l980s during the Reagan era. He played a key role in implementing the first stage of financial deregulation, which was conducive to mass bankruptcies, mergers and acquisitions. This led up to the October 19, 1987 stock market crash. He has had a long association with the Rockefeller family via his positions at Chase Bank and his membership to the Trilateral Commission, of which he was a founding member. Mr. Volker also holds a membership of the Trust Committee of Rockefeller Group, Inc. (RGI), which he joined in 1987.

Timothy Geithner was the CEO of the Federal Reserve Bank of New York. He also served as Vice Chairman of the Federal Open Market Committee (FOMC)—which plays an important role in shaping monetary policy. Gaithner was also a former Clinton administration Treasury official. He has worked for Henry Kissinger at Kissinger Associates and has also held a senior position at the IMF. He is a member of the Council on Foreign Relations as a Senior Fellow in the International Economics Department.

What a lovely bunch!!

The people that were on Obama's list of potential cabinet members all had nearly the same background. Most of these characters belong to the same think-tank groups as the aforementioned darlings. Obama has preached CHANGE, but he is recycling the same old garbage that has already passed through the White House. His list of potentials is filled with bankers or people with a background in banking. Clearly Obama is in office because Wall Street helped to put him there.

REUTERS UK

Wall Street puts its money behind Obama

Thu Jun 5, 2008 10:50am BST

By Emily Kaiser

WASHINGTON (Reuters) - Wall Street is putting its money behind Democrat Barack Obama for president, despite ***worries that his administration would raise taxes and take a tougher line on trade and regulation****. The signs Wall Street reads point to Democrats prevailing in the November presidential and general election as voters punish the incumbent Republican Party for a flagging economy and lengthy Iraq war. And the fact that Obama began raking in a bigger share of the cash as his campaign picked up steam suggests that investors simply want to back the eventual winner. Illinois Sen. Obama, who captured the Democratic presidential nomination on Tuesday after a lengthy primary battle against New York Sen. Hillary Clinton, has received $7.9 million (4.1 million pounds) n contributions from the securities and investment industries, according to the Center for Responsive Politics. His opponent, Republican Sen. John McCain of Arizona, banked a little under $4.2 million, putting him behind fellow Republicans Rudolph Giuliani and Mitt Romney, who have long since dropped out of the race.*

Read the entire article at:
http://uk.reuters.com/article/stocksNews/idUKNOA53525520080605

Now the Obama administration has introduced a financial bailout that is greater than the one proposed by the Bush administration. They are very deceptive. The Obama administration has many believing that their $787 billion bailout is for the people—not the bankers. Let us do simple mathematics to figure out whether there is a chance that this money is for the people. According to the October 6, 2008 press release by the U.S. Census Bureau, the nation's housing stock is at about 128 million. If this money was for the people, you would divide the $787 billion by the amount of total existing housing units ($787,000,000,000 ÷ 128,000,000= $6,148). The extra $6,000 per household would stimulate the economy. People would either spend it, thereby putting it back into the real economy,[66] or save it and boost the financial economy.[67] Instead, they are allocating $90 billion dollars in infrastructure spending, $54 billion to boost energy production from renewable sources, $87 billion in medical care for low-income people, $79 billion to help schools and colleges prevent cutbacks, and by the time they get to you, they have a refundable $500 dollar tax credit. This means the people are only going to see a measly 9% of Obama's $787 billion so-called bailout. (These are only the preliminary numbers).

What is a family, who is struggling to pay their mortgage, going to do with $500? I will tell you what that family is going to do. They are going to default on their mortgage and lose their home. The people, whose homes are in foreclosure, do not understand how all of this bailout stuff was originally supposed to help them. Most of the $700 billion given out by Bush is gone and Obama's package[68] offers very little, if any, relief for struggling home owners. Instead, they are telling you (straight up) that the money is going to be invested to maintain the slavery. Whenever they talk about infrastructure, education, and things like energy, they are looking to tighten the grip on the people. Think about it! The government must believe that we (the slaves) cannot fund these things through the

---

[66] The real economy consists of goods and services. The financial economy (banking and investing) is purposely designed to thwart and suppress the real economy.

[67] The more money people save, the more reserves banks have available to lend. Unfortunately, fractional reserve banking is a part of our monetary system. I contend that it is the intentional abuse of fractional reserve banking that is a detriment to our economy. In rare cases where it may be used to stimulate the economy, fractional reserve banking may serve as a positive monetary tool. The 10 to 14% reserve requirements are the harmful features of fractional reserve banking.

[68] Obama's stimulus package is beginning to look more like an investment than a bailout or anything else.

natural course of spending and investing. They feel the need to take the money from us (via taxes) and fund these sectors themselves. All they are doing is staying on the path of overspending and devaluing the currency by flooding the market with more fed notes. This could only lead to a higher rate of inflation due to the fact that there are currently less goods and services in the economy (based on the rise in unemployment).

The fact that they are desperately trying to implode the dollar is in plain site for anyone to see. If the excessive spending by the Bush administration helped get us to this point, how can the Obama administration believe that they can borrow and spend their way out of this recession/ depression? NO WAY POSSIBLE!!!! But they know this. This is all being done by design. If Bush was still in office and proposed an additional bailout for even more money, everyone would have been in an uproar. The bait and switch trick has everyone cheering Obama for the same exact things they attacked Bush for doing.

According to some media reports, the Obama bill would provide for $550 billion in job-creating investments over a two year period and $275 billion dollars in tax relief. This package is very backward and illogical. Whoever devised this plan should be put in jail for stupidity. From where do these people believe the government acquires money? They obviously are not aware that the government feeds off of the tax paying slaves. If they understood this, they would know that the $550 billion is money that was either; already collected from taxes (personal, excise, corporate, etc.), or will be collected after the government borrows to fund the investments. Either way, the $550 billion is still going to be a liability to the American taxpayer. The reader is probably thinking that it has to be more complicated than that. But it is not! Think of a mob boss who always comes around your place of business to get his 20% cut. One day he is feeling generous so he decides to give you back 5% of the money he has unjustly taken from you. Do you see the con game?

The Subprime Mortgage Crisis Explained

The criminal elite control the game of money and banking. They know that pumping all this money into the U.S. economy is only going to keep the value of the dollar in a downward spiral. It has been a process of dollar devaluation. They do things that only appear to be credible. In reality, the goal is to make sure the economy and the dollar collapse in the same theatrical manner as Enron. If they stop dropping interest rates and discontinue pumping more Fed notes (dollars) into the economy, we may only have a recession. But a recession is not good enough for these criminals. They want a depression. Historically, what comes with a depression? A depression brings forth consolidation and regulation. The consolidation of banks and other financial institutions mean more centralized power. The goal is to get the decision making process into the hands of the few. And what will accomplish such a feat? For starters, new laws to give them "in your face" control and power.

The phony bailout bill is nothing more than another complicated form of imposing a tax on the people. We are not the cause of the economic disaster, but we will bare the burden of it. We have been hoodwinked and bamboozled into thinking that the economy is tanking because of the subprime mortgage crisis. That is utterly absurd! If it were true, they would have at least pretended to use the $700 billion for that purpose! Instead, reports have surfaced stating that the banks are going to use the bailout money to buy other financial institutions, pay dividends, increase their employees pay, give executives a bonus, or will simply hold on to the money until an opportunity comes along.

Was there a mortgage crisis? Yes, there was a crisis. However, that is only one corner of the economy. Sophisticated loan sharks created that collapse, and the

Adjustable-Rate Mortgage (ARM)[69] loan was the instrument used to cause it.

The ARM loan was the guiding force behind the mortgage bubble. The subprime mortgage crisis was purposely engineered. To understand how, we need to understand the nature of the ARM loan. Contrary to popular beliefs, most people who received these loans were qualified applicants. However, they were only qualified to make payments at the initial interest rate. An ARM loan starts with a relatively lower interest rate that appeals to the borrowers. In a matter of years (depending upon the note), the interest the borrower pays is reset to a higher rate. In most cases, it resets to a rate that is significantly higher than the initial interest rate. This is what pushed many home owners out of qualification status and into foreclosure. The number of people who defaulted on their mortgages exploded in 2005 and 2006. Naturally, this increased the number of houses on the market. The oversupply of houses and lack of buyers caused the house prices to plunge in late 2006 and early 2007.

In the past, mortgages were held by small local banks. These local banks had a real interest in working with their borrowers to make sure that everything possible was being done to pay back the loans. However, in the current situation, mortgages have been sold, resold, and pooled together into securities. These securities are then sold to investors in the financial markets. These so-called securities are toxic. They are worthless bundles of paper created by financial institutions. The bailout bill has authorized the Treasury Department to purchase these worthless securities with your tax dollars. The Treasury is not purchasing mortgage notes! If they were, it wouldn't be as detrimental because the notes would still have the value of the property.

---

[69] A mortgage loan whose interest rate fluctuates according to the movements of an assigned index or designated market indicator—such as the weekly average of one-year US Treasury Bills—over the life of the loan.

Associated Press

Uses for $700 billion bailout money ever shifting

Saturday October 25, 10:53 am ET
By John Dunbar, Associated Press Writer

Treasury tacks on uses for $700 billion bailout money with shifting economic winds

WASHINGTON (AP) -- First, the $700 billion rescue for the economy was about buying devalued mortgage-backed securities from tottering banks to unclog frozen credit markets. Then it was about using $250 billion of it to buy stakes in banks. The idea was that banks would use the money to start making loans again.

But reports surfaced that bankers might instead use the money to buy other banks, pay dividends, give employees a raise and executives a bonus, or just sit on it. Insurance companies now want a piece; maybe automakers, too, even though Congress has approved $25 billion in low-interest loans for them. Three weeks after becoming law, and with the first dollar of the $700 billion yet to go out, officials are just beginning to talk about helping a few strapped homeowners keep the foreclosure wolf from the door.

As the crisis worsens, the government's reaction keeps changing. Lawmakers in both parties are starting to gripe that the bailout is turning out to be far different from what the Bush administration sold to Congress. In buying equity stakes in banks, the Treasury has "deviated significantly from its original course," says Alabama Sen. Richard Shelby, the top Republican on the Senate Banking, Housing and Urban Affairs Committee. "We need to examine closely the reason for this change," said Shelby, who opposed the bailout.

The centerpiece of the Emergency Economic Stabilization Act is the "troubled asset relief program," or TARP for short. Critics note that tarps are used to cover things up. The money was to be devoted to buying "toxic" mortgage-backed securities whose value has fallen in lockstep with home prices. But once European governments said they were going into the banking business, Treasury Secretary Henry Paulson followed suit and diverted $250 billion to buy stock in healthy banks to spur lending.

Bank executives hinted they might instead use it for acquisitions. Sen. Christopher Dodd, chairman of the Senate banking committee, said this development was "beyond troubling." Sure enough, a day after Dodd, D-Conn., made the comment, the government confirmed that PNC Financial Services Group Inc. was approved to receive $7.7 billion in return for company stock. At the same time, PNC said it was acquiring National City Corp. for $5.58 billion.

"Although there will be some consolidation, that's not the driver behind this program," Paulson recently told PBS talk show host Charlie Rose. "The driver is to have our healthy banks be well-capitalized so that they can play the role they need to play for our country right now." Other planned uses of the bailout money have lawmakers protesting, although it is only fair to note there is nothing in the law that they just wrote to prevent those uses.

Sen. Charles Schumer, D-N.Y. questioned allowing banks that accept bailout bucks to continue paying dividends on their common stock. "There are far better uses of taxpayer dollars than continuing dividend payments to shareholders," he said.

Schumer, whose constituents include Wall Street bankers, said he also fears that they might stuff the money "under the proverbial mattress" rather than make loans.

Neel Kashkari, head of the Treasury's financial stability program, told Dodd's committee this past week that there are few strings attached to the capital-infusion program because too many rules would discourage financial institutions from participating. As the bank plan has become a priority, the effort to buy troubled assets has receded from the headlines. Potential conflicts of interest pose all kinds of problems in finding qualified companies to manage that program.

"Firms with the relevant financial expertise may also hold assets that become eligible for sale into the TARP or represent clients who hold troubled assets," Kashkari said. The challenge was made plain when the Treasury hired the Bank of New York Mellon Corp. as "custodian" of the troubled assets purchase program. The bank will conduct "reverse auctions" to buy the toxic securities on behalf of the Treasury. The lower the price they set, the better chance sellers have of getting rid of the devalued securities.

On the same day it hired Mellon, the Treasury also picked the company to receive a $3 billion investment as part of the capital-infusion program. The same bank hired to help manage part of the economic rescue plan became a beneficiary of it. With the Nov. 4 election nearing, lawmakers decided it was important to remind the government officials running the bailout program about parts of the law aimed at helping distressed homeowners by offering federal guarantees to mortgages renegotiated down to lower monthly payments.

"The key to our nation's economic recovery is the recovery of the housing market," Dodd said. "And the key to recovery of the housing market is reducing foreclosures." Sheila Bair, who heads the Federal Deposit Insurance Corp., responded that her agency is working "closely and creatively" with Treasury officials to "realize the potential benefits of this authority."

http://biz.yahoo.com/ap/081025/meltdown_evolving_bailout.html

The American people need to understand that the collapse of the economy (and dollar) was not due to the subprime mortgage crisis. They only used that in order to delegate the blame away from themselves and onto the American people. If we are the cause of the collapse, then psychologically it makes the situation acceptable. The bankers can then justifiably be bailed out with our tax dollars. This is so outlandish and insulting to anyone who looks at the data. According to RealtyTrac.com, during 2007 nearly 1.3 million properties in the U.S. were subject to foreclosure activity. This was an astounding 79% jump from 2006. Let us do a little math shall we? If we divide $700 billion dollars by the number of homes in default (1.3 million), this would equal $538,461 per property. Keep in mind that the average mortgage in the United States does not equal $500,000 dollars. According to the National Association of Realtors, the actual numbers are closer to about $250,000. These numbers are nauseating. If the $700 billion bailout money was given to the people instead of the bankers, then the bankers would get their money and the mortgagor (borrower) would no longer be in default. This would instantly correct the housing market and give a boost to the credit markets. But of course, the bailout was not designed to boost the economy or help people with their mortgages. It is about hijacking the Treasury Department and bringing in a new financial order.

A lawyer for the Cato Institute[70] named Robert A. Levy wrote an article for the Legal Times entitled; "Is the bailout constitutional?" In the article, Mr. Levy states, "The federal government has no constitutional authority to spend taxpayers' money to buy distressed assets, much less to take an ownership position in private financial institutions."

***Sources for Housing data*:**
http://www.census.gov/const/uspriceann.pdf
http://www.realestateabc.com/outlook/overall.htm

---

[70] The Cato Institute is a libertarian think tank headquartered in Washington, D.C.

THE FRAUD OF MONEY AND BANKING

CHAPTER VII.

A BANKERS COUP D' ETAT

"The modern banking system manufactures money out of nothing. The process is perhaps the most astounding piece of sleight of hand that was ever invented. Banking was conceived in inequity and born in sin. Bankers own the earth. Take it away from them but leave them the power to create money, and with a flick of a pen, they will create enough money to buy it back again. Take this great power away from them and all great fortunes like mine will disappear, for then this would be a better and happier world to live in. But if you want to continue to be the slaves of bankers and pay the cost of your own slavery, then let bankers continue to create money and control credit"

-Sir Josiah Stamp, president of the Bank of England and the second richest man in Britain in the 1920s, speaking at the University of Texas in 1927.

This is a profound statement coming from a former President of the Bank of England. The statement ties into the fact that all booms and busts in the economy are not by happenstance. The big banks make loans to boost the economy (making money available) and then tighten the money supply to make money scarce. This is the same strategy they have been using since before the great depression. Everyone is familiar with the roaring twenties. In those days the economy appeared to be as healthy as ever. The Federal Reserve Act had been passed during the previous decade, everyone was dancing, and things were looking sweet. Nevertheless, shortly after its creation the Federal Reserve System (by the FOMC) quickly set out policies to loosen the money supply. The loosening of the money supply, if abused, can create an environment of excessive credit. Excessive credit then leads to an overpriced stock market. Within ten short years of the Federal Reserve's creation, the central bank flow of credit overpriced the U.S. stock market. Subsequently after the collapse of the stock market in 1929, the world entered its first official great depression in 1933.

The key is to get people to live well above their means. Once upon a time, most people did not buy homes, farms, and expensive things on credit. Most people used their savings or inheritance to purchase these items. Another important thing was the fact that most people mastered a trait and opened their own businesses. During the 1800s, most people did not depend on corporations for jobs. They either owned their own company or worked for a proprietorship (usually owned by someone familiar). Today we rely on the big corporations to give us jobs. Unfortunately the corporations are nothing but an extension of the banks. In this day and time, we are dependent on the banks and corporations to take care of us. This basically means that we are at their mercy for employment.

The criminal elite always need us to be dependent on something. In the old world order structure, we were dependent on religion to give us instructions on how to live our lives and what we should believe. The slave has to always be kept dependent of his master and made to believe that the life he lives is the best available. The slave must also be made to believe that he cannot fend for himself. Only the slave master can provide for the slave. The slave master offers the slave the illusion that he is in the best possible scenario. The slave's only job is to remain a slave so that he may enjoy the scenario. The slave could never be told the truth. This is why a slave could never be taught how to read. In elementary school we were taught that during slavery a slave was not allowed to learn how to read and write. The Unknowns understand this concept because they created it. They are so deceptively clever. Through their propaganda and false educational system, they have you believing that you know how to read. In order to deceive you into believing that you are not a slave, they had to first teach that if you could sound out the words written on a piece of paper, it means you could read. I understand that this idea sounds peculiar and absurd. But what we need to understand is the following. Simply because you can pronounce written words does not mean you understand them. For example, if you read your mortgage note or credit card agreement and you do not understand the sounds that came out of your mouth (or heard in your head), then you are considered to be at the same level as the person who cannot pronounce the written words. Neither one of you know what the words mean.

This is why they make everything complicated. In order to keep the people in a state of confusion, they have to create a language within a language. The doctors are intelligent but they do not understand law, the lawyers are intelligent but they do not understand medicine, physicists are intelligent but they do not understand law or medicine, etc. This is done purposely to maintain the chaos. This is symbolic of the biblical story of Babel.[71] As long as everyone is out doing their own thing they will never come together for a common cause.

---

[71] The story of the Tower of Babel is found in the book of Genesis of the Bible, under chapter eleven. In this story, the people were united and spoke one language. Their language was broken up into many dialects and tongues by god in order to create confusion. The confusion was created to stop the progress of creating a tower that would reach the heavens.

Glass-Steagall Act of 1933

The Glass-Steagall Act of 1933 was passed in an attempt to separate the nationwide commercial bank failures of the Great Depression. The act was named after two members of Congress, Senator Carter Glass and Representative Henry Steagall.[72] The Act separated investment and commercial banking activities. Many economists and financial analysts blamed the 1929 stock market crash on improper banking activities. Commercial Banks simply took on too much risk with demand deposits (customer's money). Banks were investing their assets and lending money at very high rates. Naturally, companies began to default on some of the loans. This caused a domino affect. For example, if corporation A is doing business with corporation B, and corporation B goes out of business, corporation A must find another company to do business with. However, as the number of players dwindles, it cost more to do business with other companies. This is the simple science of supply and demand. As companies began to fail and people became unemployed, costumers went to their banks to withdraw funds. As funds were being withdrawn, the banks had less and less demand deposits to invest and lend. Therefore, bank runs[73] became common. As banks started to fall one by one, anyone with money in those banks was basically ruined.

---

[72] Senator Carter Glass, a former U.S. Treasury Secretary and the founder of the U.S. Federal Reserve System, was the primary force behind the GSA. Henry Bascom Steagall was a House of Representatives member and chairman of the House Banking and Currency Committee.

[73] A bank run (also known as a run on the bank) occurs when a large number of bank depositors withdraw their deposits because they believe the bank is going to fail.

In May of 1956, the *Bank Holding Company Act* was passed, extending the restrictions on banks. The Act included that bank holding companies owning two or more banks were prohibited from engaging in non-banking activities and acquiring out of state banks. There is no question that some of these laws are passed by people with good intentions. However, most of the laws only affect the smaller institutions.[74] The international banking cartels are never affected because they are the ones calling the real shots. And whenever they wish to create chaos in the economy, they sick the smaller banks on the people. This current collapse is a prime example. In November of 1999, Congress repealed the Glass-Steagall Act of 1933 with the enactment of the Gramm-Leach-Bliley Act. This new act eliminated the Glass-Steagall's restrictions against affiliations between commercial and investment banks. Furthermore, the Gramm-Leach-Bliley Act allows banking institutions to provide a broader range of services, including underwriting and other investment dealing activities. Naturally, this increased credit.

Large economic recessions are, almost always, caused by the issuance of excessive credit. Credit is the key to creating the booms and the busts in the economy. They issue excessive credit in order to get you to live above your means. Then, when they wish to engineer an economic collapse or slow down, they make credit hard to come by. Only during a credit crunch do the people realize that they have been living above their means. What are all those people who depended on credit cards going to do when no credit card company will accept their business?

During times of economic prosperity, investment banks usually make their most volatile and most speculative investments. The great collapse of the financial mar-

---

[74] The smaller institutions even include the likes of a Merrill Lynch and Washington Mutual. These are relatively small players in the great scheme of things. The international banking cartels are comprised of your central banks, including the International Monetary Fund and the World Bank.

kets during the Great Depression of the 1930s was no different.

Today the credit derivatives market, better known as credit default swaps,[75] have played a major role in the economic implosion. These are the types of securities that banks have pledged to the government in exchange for bailout money. What are these derivatives and credit swaps? They are best described as legal bets placed on certain stocks and bonds. The buyer of the security pays a premium and in return receives a sum of money if he wins the bet. The seller wins if nothing happens during the term of the bet. Credit Default Swaps (CDS) are the cornerstone of the credit derivatives market. These derivatives account for more than 98 percent of all credit derivatives. The underlying theory of how these securities work is equal to the concept of buying insurance for something that you do not own. For instance, it is like buying property insurance for a building that you do not own. However you still collect the full value of the building if it burns to the ground. These securities have been a cash cow on Wall Street since the Glass-Steagall Act was repealed in 1999.

According to the Office of the Comptroller of the Currency, JPMorgan, Citigroup Inc., and Bank of America held 92 percent of all the disclosed credit derivative contracts. However, this number is only an estimate. This market is practically unregulated and the contracts are private—therefore, not easily measured.

---

[75] Investopedia (a Forbes digital company) explains *Credit Default Swap - (CDS)...* as;

The buyer of a credit swap receives credit protection, whereas the seller of the swap guarantees the credit worthiness of the product. By doing this, the risk of default is transferred from the holder of the fixed income security to the seller of the swap. For example, the buyer of a credit swap will be entitled to the par value of the bond by the seller of the swap, should the bond default in its coupon payments.

The buyer of a Credit Default Swap does not need to own the underlying security; in fact the buyer does not even have to suffer a loss from the event of a default.

The Great Swindle

On September 10, 2001 (the day before the 9/11 Terror Attacks), it was reported that about $2.3 trillion dollars were missing from the Pentagon. How lucky were the thieves that al-Qaeda[76] decided to attack the very next day? And of course, after the attacks this missing money was forgotten. You cannot make this stuff up! I am surprised they did not blame the missing money on al-Qaeda. We are not talking about pennies here. We are talking about $8,000 dollars per every man, woman, and child in the United States. A family of five would equal $40,000. What would you do with $40,000? Think about this. If we would not have relinquished this money by way of paying taxes, this would have been $2.3 trillion dollars that would have been infused into the real economy. If this is not a severe mis-handling of our hard-earned tax dollars, then what is? How is it possible that trillions upon trillions of dollars continually come up missing? Pentagon auditors are baffled and do not have a clue as to how the military cannot account for 25% of the money it spends.

On September 10, 2001, old Donald Rumsfeld admitted to the press that "According to some estimates, we cannot track $2.3 trillion in transactions." Again, we are not talking about $2.30 cents here. How can they not know what happened to $2.3 TRILLION DOLLARS! Instead of worrying about al-Qaeda, we need to start worrying about al-Criminals in Washington. After 9/11, the Bush administration's suggested 2003 budget called for a $48 billion dollars in defense spending. If 25% of the $48 billion is lost as usual, we are talking about another $12 billion dollars down the tubes. This is another head scratcher. The same criminals who stole $2.3 trillion were now set to benefit from the War on Terror. Who in their right mind would give these people more money? These are staggering numbers

[76] At first, al-Qaeda was also being accused of buying put options on United and American Airlines. This is important because put options are basically bets that the stock price will fall.

considering the fact that the government is suppose to show transparency with how our tax dollars are being spent. This is pure and clear lawlessness on the part of these criminals. The U. S. Constitution (article I. § 9) clearly states: *"No money shall be drawn from the treasury, but in consequence of appropriations made by law."* Bills for appropriating money originate in the House of Representatives, but may be amended in the Senate. How can they finance programs that have not been approved by Congress? The key is their continual production of unreliable financial statements as well as failing to publish required independent annual audited financial statements. These atrocities are spun as government and bureaucratic incompetence. Meanwhile, the real wealth of the country continues to move from the lower and middle classes up to the wealthiest two-percent.

Billions upon billions of dollars are spent without any oversight from Congress or any other authority. And yet, they continue to collect taxes from us. They use fancy words such as "Budget" and "Deficit" without ever qualifying their meaning. This way, they can deceive you into believing that if they go over budget, it is a precedence to hike up taxes.

The word budget is usually defined as; *An itemized summary of estimated or intended expenditures for a given period along with proposals for financing them.* In simple terms, it only means that if I made a $100,000, but I only wanted to spend $10,000 of it for the next two months, I have created a budget. If I go over $10,000, it does not mean that I am broke! It does not mean that I should pick up extra hours at work. It only means that I went over my intention of only spending $10,000. This is what the government does at all levels, whether at the federal, state, or local. They bring in trillions, billions, and millions of dollars. Then, they give the people an estimate of what they would like to spend out of that total. When they surpass the estimate, they make a big to-do about it in order to sucker the people into paying more taxes.

CBS NEWS

The War On Waste

Defense Department Cannot Account For 25% Of Funds — $2.3 Trillion

LOS ANGELES, Jan. 29, 2002

CBS) *On Sept. 10, Secretary of Defense Donald Rumsfeld declared war. Not on foreign terrorists, "the adversary's closer to home. It's the Pentagon bureaucracy," he said.*

He said money wasted by the military poses a serious threat.

"In fact, it could be said it's a matter of life and death," he said.

Rumsfeld promised change but the next day – Sept. 11-- the world changed and in the rush to fund the war on terrorism, the war on waste seems to have been forgotten.

Just last week President Bush announced, "my 2003 budget calls for more than $48 billion in new defense spending."

More money for the Pentagon, ***CBS News Correspondent Vince Gonzales*** *reports, while its own auditors admit the military cannot account for 25 percent of what it spends.*

"According to some estimates we cannot track $2.3 trillion in transactions," Rumsfeld admitted.

$2.3 trillion — that's $8,000 for every man, woman and child in America. To understand how the Pentagon can lose track of trillions, consider the case of one military accountant who tried to find out what happened to a mere $300 million.

"We know it's gone. But we don't know what they spent it on," said Jim Minnery, Defense Finance and Accounting Service.

Minnery, a former Marine turned whistle-blower, is risking his job by speaking out for the first time about the millions he noticed were missing from one defense agency's balance sheets. Minnery tried to follow the money trail, even crisscrossing the country looking for records.

"The director looked at me and said 'Why do you care about this stuff?' It took me aback, you know? My supervisor asking me why I care about doing a good job," said Minnery.

He was reassigned and says officials then covered up the problem by just writing it off.

"They have to cover it up," he said. "That's where the corruption comes in. They have to cover up the fact that they can't do the job."

The Pentagon's Inspector General "partially substantiated" several of Minnery's allegations but could not prove officials tried "to manipulate the financial statements."

Twenty years ago, Department of Defense Analyst Franklin C. Spinney made headlines exposing what he calls the "accounting games." He's still there, and although he does not speak for the Pentagon, he believes the problem has gotten worse.

"Those numbers are pie in the sky. The books are cooked routinely year after year," he said.

Another critic of Pentagon waste, Retired Vice Admiral Jack Shanahan, commanded the Navy's 2nd Fleet the first time Donald Rumsfeld served as Defense Secretary, in 1976.

In his opinion, "With good financial oversight we could find $48 billion in loose change in that building, without having to hit the taxpayers."

Refer to:
http://www.cbsnews.com/stories/2002/01/29/eveningnews/main325985.shtml

All of this took place despite the fact that Donald Rumsfeld's office, on July 19, 2001, issued a memorandum establishing the Department Wide Financial Modernization Program. The purpose of the program was supposedly to ensure reliable, accurate, and timely financial management information upon which to make effective management decisions.

***Refer to*: http://www.dodig.osd.mil/Audit/reports/fy02/02-055.pdf**

As they say, "So much for that." Where are the checks and balances to avoid this robbery? Would you believe that there is not now, or ever has been a criminal investigation concerning this missing money? What would happen if the accountant of your company failed to pass an audit like this? Heck, what would happen if a citizen failed an IRS audit like this? (Gun barrel time!)

The most disturbing thing about this robbery is the fact that the Defense Department received a substantial amount of funding after the 9/11 Terror Attacks. Another disturbing tid-bit is the fact that no one has an idea of what they spent the money on. These are your tax dollars we are talking about. The same tax dollars that have been swindled by the banks. The banker bailout bill was nothing more than a financial terror attack on the American people. Now we have the Federal Reserve and the Treasury Department making private deals with the big banks they were suppose to bailout. The Federal Reserve and the former Secretary of the Treasury, Henry Paulson,[77] refuse to tell the American people what bank is getting what, and what securities the banks are giving the government. The Fed has given this money to the banks under the authority of programs that were put in place about a year and a half ago. They intentionally put these programs in place before they completely blew up the economy. These demons are cunning and ruthless.

In order to get a decent understanding of how criminal these people are, we need to examine the fact that Bloomberg News (a major financial news company) asked the Federal Reserve to disclose the names of the banks that are getting special Fed financial help. The Fed refused to disclose the names of the banks and the securities the banks are handing over (pledging).

---

[77] Prior to joining Goldman Sachs, Paulson was a member of the White House Domestic Council, serving as Staff Assistant to the president from 1972 to 1973, and as Staff Assistant to the Assistant Secretary of Defense at the Pentagon from 1970 to 1972.

Los Angeles Times

Bloomberg sues to get list of banks borrowing from the Fed

12:10 PM, November 10, 2008

*Should the **Federal Reserve** have to disclose the names of the banks and other companies that are getting special Fed financial help? Bloomberg News thinks so. And because the Fed won't tell, the news organization now is suing for the information.*

From a Bloomberg story today:

*The Federal Reserve is refusing to identify the recipients of almost $2 trillion of emergency loans from American taxpayers or the troubled assets the central bank is accepting as collateral. Fed Chairman **Ben S. Bernanke** and Treasury Secretary **Henry M. Paulson** said in September they would comply with congressional demands for transparency in a $700 billion bailout of the banking system. Two months later, as the Fed lends far more than that in separate rescue programs that didn't require approval by Congress, Americans have no idea where their money is going or what securities the banks are pledging in return. Bloomberg News has requested details of the Fed lending under the U.S. Freedom of Information Act and filed a federal lawsuit Nov. 7 seeking to force disclosure. The Fed made the loans under terms of 11 programs, eight of them created in the past 15 months, in the midst of the biggest financial crisis since the Great Depression. Federal Reserve spokeswoman*

Michelle Smith declined to comment on the loans or the Bloomberg lawsuit. Treasury spokeswoman Michele Davis didn't respond to a phone call and an e-mail seeking comment.

The Fed, of course, can argue that it has a good reason for keeping borrowers' identities secret: It doesn't want to risk another banking panic by giving stock traders and depositors a list of institutions that would immediately be seen as the weakest links in the financial chain. No regulator wants to force a failure if there's a decent chance an institution could survive, with time.

From the Bloomberg story: Banks oppose any release of information because it might signal weakness and spur short-selling or a run by depositors, said Scott Talbott, senior vice president of government affairs for the Financial Services Roundtable, a Washington trade group. "You have to balance the need for transparency with protecting the public interest," Talbott said. "Taxpayers have a right to know where their tax dollars are going, but one piece of information standing alone could undermine public confidence in the system."

Source: http://latimesblogs.latimes.com/money_co/2008/11/should-the-fede.html

Under the leadership of Fed Bank Chairman Ben S. Bernanke and the head of the Treasury Department, Henry Paulson, a deal was made with Congress in which both men agreed that their agencies would comply with congressional demands for transparency concerning the bailout. Now, after rushing the bill through Congress and after lending far more than $700 billion, both the Federal Reserve and the Treasury Department are committing treachery against the people. By denying the promised disclosure of where the money was going, and which securities have been pledged by the banks, these people have betrayed the tax-paying public.

Bloomberg.com

Fed Defies Transparency Aim in Refusal to Disclose

By Mark Pittman, Bob Ivry and Alison Fitzgerald

Nov. 10 (Bloomberg) -- The Federal Reserve is refusing to identify the recipients of almost $2 trillion of emergency loans from American taxpayers or the troubled assets the central bank is accepting as collateral.

Fed Chairman Ben S. Bernanke and Treasury Secretary Henry Paulson said in September they would comply with congressional demands for transparency in a $700 billion bailout of the banking system. Two months later, as the Fed lends far more than that in separate rescue programs that didn't require approval by Congress, Americans have no idea where their money is going or what securities the banks are pledging in return.

Refer to: http://www.bloomberg.com/apps/news?pid=20601087&sid=aatlky_cH.tY&refer=worldwide

I am not more intelligent than the lawyers at Bloomberg News, however, one thing that those lawyers might overlook is the fact that the Federal Reserve could claim they are not a government agency. The Federal Reserve is a private institution that has government oversight—same as any investment bank. Therefore, since they do not have publicly traded stock, the Freedom of Information Act may not apply in this case. In the case of *Lewis v. the United States*, the court ruled that it lacked subject-matter jurisdiction[78] to rule in the case because "Federal Reserve Banks are not federal instrumentalities for purposes of the Act, but are independent, privately owned and locally controlled corporations."

---

[78] A court has subject matter jurisdiction when it has the authority to hear a case that has all the elements necessary to empower the court to give relief to the complaining party. For example, if you file suit in tax court, but your complaint is that the defendant hit you with his car, the court lacks subject matter jurisdiction to rule favorably for the plaintiff.

Lewis v. United States, 680 F.2d 1239 (1982)

John L. Lewis, Plaintiff/Appellant,
v.
United States of America, Defendant/Appellee.

No. 80-5905
United States Court of Appeals, Ninth Circuit.
Submitted March 2, 1982.
Decided April 19, 1982.
As Amended June 24, 1982.

Plaintiff, who was injured by vehicle owned and operated by a federal reserve bank, brought action alleging jurisdiction under the Federal Tort Claims Act. The United States District Court for the Central District of California, David W. Williams, J., dismissed holding that federal reserve bank was not a federal agency within meaning of Act and that the court therefore lacked subject-matter jurisdiction. Appeal was taken. The Court of Appeals, Poole, Circuit Judge, held that federal reserve banks are not federal instrumentalities for purposes of the Act, but are independent, privately owned and locally controlled corporations.

Affirmed.

1. United States

There are no sharp criteria for determining whether an entity is a federal agency within meaning of the Federal Tort Claims Act, but critical factor is existence of federal government control over "detailed physical performance" and "day to day operation" of an entity. . . .

2. United States

Federal reserve banks are not federal instrumentalities for purposes of a Federal Tort Claims Act, but are independent, privately owned and locally controlled corporations in light of fact that direct supervision and control of each bank is exercised by board of directors, federal reserve banks, though heavily regulated, are locally controlled by their member banks, banks are listed neither as "wholly owned" government corporations nor as "mixed ownership" corporations; federal reserve banks receive no appropriated funds from Congress and the banks are empowered to sue and be sued in their own names. . . .

3. United States

Under the Federal Tort Claims Act, federal liability is narrowly based on traditional agency principles and does not necessarily lie when a tortfeasor simply works for an entity, like the Reserve Bank, which performs important activities for the government. . . .

Sources: http://cases.justia.com/us-court-of-appeals/F2/680/1239/200393/
http://caselaw.lp.findlaw.com/cgi-bin/getcase.pl?court=7th&navby=case&no=012522

The Good Politician

If any well meaning politician investigates and attempts to go up against the banking cartels, they will be dealt with. Remember Eliot Spitzer? If he had cooperated with the banker takeover fraud, do you believe hookers would have been an issue? Are we to believe that the major news media was so inept as to forego the blatantly obvious correlation between the out of the ordinary federal law enforcement investigation, and the coincidental leak about the private life of the former governor? The news media conveniently failed to cover the details of Spitzer's public charges against the Bush administration and the national banking system. Spitzer was exposing part of the scam shortly before this alleged scandal broke loose.

According to reports, Spitzer came into the FBI's crosshairs when a bank reported to the IRS that a significant amount of money had been "suspiciously" transferred from one account to another. Apparently, they were working on bringing Mr. Spitzer down for over a year. This is why they have created all of the legal spying laws. Did you know that if you are a wealthy person and you move as little as $5,000, your bank will inform the IRS, who in-turn informs the FBI? Doesn't this sound a bit much to catch a guy with some hookers? Laws such as The Bank Secrecy Act are used as tools to spy on the American people. According to the FBI, there are terrorists lurking around every corner waiting to kill Americans. If the FBI and the White House believe that hype, why is the FBI wasting valuable time and resources investigating guys who hire expensive call girls? These demons like to play these tricks on us. Did you know that in the State of Nevada prostitution is legal? You can get a license to be a hooker in Nevada. What is a license? A license is nothing but a "permission" to do something. Otherwise, you are breaking the law.

***Source for Spitzer raid*:**
http://www.cnn.com/2008/POLITICS/03/11/spitzer.money/index.html

washingtonpost.com

Predatory Lenders' Partner in Crime

How the Bush Administration Stopped the States From Stepping In to Help Consumers

By **Eliot Spitzer**
Thursday, February 14, 2008; Page A25

Several years ago, state attorneys general and others involved in consumer protection began to notice a marked increase in a range of predatory lending practices by mortgage lenders. Some were misrepresenting the terms of loans, making loans without regard to consumers' ability to repay, making loans with deceptive "teaser" rates that later ballooned astronomically, packing loans with undisclosed charges and fees, or even paying illegal kickbacks. These and other practices, we noticed, were having a devastating effect on home buyers. In addition, the widespread nature of these practices, if left unchecked, threatened our financial markets.

Even though predatory lending was becoming a national problem, the Bush administration looked the other way and did nothing to protect American homeowners. In fact, the government chose instead to align itself with the banks that were victimizing consumers.

Predatory lending was widely understood to present a looming national crisis. This threat was so clear that as New York attorney general, I joined with colleagues in the other 49 states in attempting to fill the void left by the federal government. Individually, and together, state attorneys general of both parties brought litigation or entered into settlements with many subprime lenders that were engaged in predatory lending practices. Several state legislatures, including New York's, enacted laws aimed at curbing such practices.

What did the Bush administration do in response? Did it reverse course and decide to take action to halt this burgeoning scourge? As Americans are now painfully aware, with hundreds of thousands of homeowners facing foreclosure and our markets reeling, the answer is a resounding no.

Not only did the Bush administration do nothing to protect consumers, it embarked on an aggressive and unprecedented campaign to prevent states from protecting their residents from the very problems to which the federal government was turning a blind eye.

Let me explain: The administration accomplished this feat through an obscure federal agency called the Office of the Comptroller of the Currency (OCC). The OCC has been in existence since the Civil War. Its mission is to ensure the fiscal soundness of national banks. For 140 years, the OCC examined the books of national banks to make sure they were balanced, an important but uncontroversial function. But a few years ago, for the first time in its history, the OCC was used as a tool against consumers.

In 2003, during the height of the predatory lending crisis, the OCC invoked a clause from the 1863 National Bank Act to issue formal opinions preempting all state predatory lending laws, thereby rendering them inoperative. The OCC also promulgated new rules that prevented states from enforcing any of their own consumer protection laws against national banks. The federal government's actions were so egregious and so unprecedented that all 50 state attorneys general, and all 50 state banking superintendents, actively fought the new rules.

But the unanimous opposition of the 50 states did not deter, or even slow, the Bush administration in its goal of protecting the banks. In fact, when my office opened an investigation of possible discrimination in mortgage lending by a number of banks, the OCC filed a federal lawsuit to stop the investigation.

Throughout our battles with the OCC and the banks, the mantra of the banks and their defenders was that efforts to curb predatory lending would deny access to credit to the very consumers the states were trying to protect. But the curbs we sought on predatory and unfair lending would have in no way jeopardized access to the legitimate credit market for appropriately priced loans. Instead, they would have stopped the scourge of predatory lending practices that have resulted in countless thousands of consumers losing their homes and put our economy in a precarious position.

When history tells the story of the subprime lending crisis and recounts its devastating effects on the lives of so many innocent homeowners, the Bush administration will not be judged favorably. The tale is still unfolding, but when the dust settles, it will be judged as a willing accomplice to the lenders who went to any lengths in their quest for profits. So willing, in fact, that it used the power of the federal government in an unprecedented assault on state legislatures, as well as on state attorneys general and anyone else on the side of consumers.

The writer is governor of New York.

Source: http://www.washingtonpost.com/wp-dyn/content/article/2008/02/13/AR2008021302783.html

In a similar fashion to Nicholas Biddle, the President of the Second Bank of the United States who threatened to bring the country into a recession if the government did not re-issue the bank's charter, Congress was threatened (with a depression) if the banker bailout bill did not pass. Dr. Michael C. Burgess, a Republican congressman from Texas, said that members of Congress were threatened with martial law[79] if the banker bill did not pass. Martial law in this case only means the suspension of normal proceedings in the House and Senate.

Dr. Burgess (R-TX) reported from the floor of the House and stated that the Republicans have been "Cut out of the process" and called unpatriotic for not blindly supporting the bi-partisan bailout. He stated "The only debate has been about what talking points to use on the American people." The most ominous revelation is when he claims that the Speaker had declared martial law. "I have been thrown out of more meetings in this capital in the last 24 hours than I ever thought possible as a duly elected representative of 825,000 citizens of north Texas", said Congressman Burgess. Burgess asked the Speaker of the House to post the bailout bill on the internet for at least 24 hours—instead of passing the largest piece of legislation in U.S. financial history "in the dark of night."

---

[79] Under the martial law procedure, long-standing House rules that require at least one day between the unveiling of significant legislation and the House floor vote on that legislation — so that members can learn what they are being asked to vote on — are swept away. Instead, under "martial law," the leadership can file legislation with tens or hundreds of pages of fine print and move immediately to debate and votes on it, before members of Congress, the media, or the public have an opportunity to understand fully what provisions have been altered or inserted into the legislation behind closed doors. This is the procedure that the leadership intends to use to muscle through important bills in the next two days.

***Source*: http://burgess.house.gov/News/DocumentSingle.aspx?DocumentID=103976**

Republican Congressman Dr. Michael C. Burgess
http://www.youtube.com/watch?v=l7B4laX1E70

Burgess: A Bailout by Any Other Name is Still a Bailout

Washington, DC, Oct 3, 2008 - This bailout bill's second verse is essentially the same as the first so I cannot support it.

Today's vote is a difficult one and there are good, well-intentioned people on both sides. Action is needed and there are some necessary tax relief measures contained within. Yet, a bailout by any other name is still a bailout. It's as if we opened up the patient, poked around the tumor, and stitched them right back up without doing anything about the cancer.

Does this bailout hold people accountable? Not the right ones. Instead, it puts the whole country on the hook for the greed and irresponsibility of a few. Is expanding the size and scope of our government really the only available answer? Should Washington subsidize the irresponsibility and arrogance of Wall Street?

The phone, fax, and email systems in my office have been deluged with overwhelming opposition to this massive, unprecedented government giveaway. People are outraged that we are in this predicament and rightly so. They want accountability and not rewards for recklessness. They don't want Washington writing blank checks that their children and grandchildren will be forced to fund.

How does this bailout prevent this from happening again? What happened to personal responsibility? These questions remain unanswered as the Congress agrees to support the largest public intervention in the private market in history.

Source:
http://burgess.house.gov/News/DocumentSingle.aspx?DocumentID=104354

The Obama Illusion

In my book, THE CONSPIRACY THEORY FRAUD, I wrote about how Oklahoma declared their sovereignty under the Tenth Amendment of the United States Constitution. I also mentioned how this was a tremendous step. Now, less than a year removed from those writings, over twenty union states are drafting resolutions to declare their sovereignty. There is no question that the federal government is out of order. And yet, the precious mainstream media refuses to report on the fact that nearly half of the states in the Union are telling the federal government to buzz-off. This is the biggest story since the Civil War! Yet many of you reading this book are only hearing about it for the first time.

***Sources*:**
CO: http://www.sweetliberty.org/tenthamend.htm
UT: http://www.dailypaul.com/node/82077
NH: http://www.gencourt.state.nh.us/legislation/2009/HCR0006.html
WA: http://apps.leg.wa.gov/billinfo/summary.aspx?year=2009&bill=4009
AZ: http://www.azleg.gov/FormatDocument.asp?inDoc=/legtext/49leg/1r/bills/hcr2024p.htm
MT: http://data.opi.mt.gov/bills/2009/billhtml/HB0246.htm
MI:http://www.legislature.mi.gov/(S(21rmjiv1sl0wvw55yxurwl55))/documents/2009-2010/Journal/House/pdf/2009-HJ-01-22-002.pdf
MO: http://www.house.mo.gov/content.aspx?info=/bills091/bills/HR212.HTM
OK: http://webserver1.lsb.state.ok.us/2009-10HB/HJR1003_int.rtf

The criminals running the United States are out of control. The twenty plus states that are declaring their Tenth Amendment rights is evidence enough. But the criminal elite are very clever. Notice how they have been trying to compare Obama to Lincoln. What did Lincoln do? He saved the Union, remember? It is psychological warfare. If Obama is like Lincoln and you love Lincoln's legacy, then you will love Obama and do as he says. It is clear that Obama is supported by all the establishment elites, and yet, his presidential campaign was allegedly for change.

***Sources for Obama/Lincoln*:**
http://www.washingtonpost.com/wpdyn/content/article/2008/11/18/AR2008111803854.html
http://www.clipsyndicate.com/video/playlist/3390/777212?cpt=8&title=hillary&wpid=2057
http://thehill.com/leading-the-news/gore-compares-obama-to-lincoln-2008-08-28.html
http://www.huffingtonpost.com/bob-burnett/obama-and-lincoln_b_94819.html

The sad part about it is that most people have been fooled by the old bait and switch. We were taught to hate Bush and blame all of the countries ills on his administration. Now, they give us Barack Obama as our savior. Black Americans have been blinded by the fact that Obama is the first black president, and white Americans have been guilt tripped into going along with the Obama agenda for fear of being called "racist." The fact of the matter is that Obama is nothing but an image for the people to see. His presence is only the illusion of change. Things will be more chaotic under Obama than they were under baby Bush.[80] There is not an agenda that was started by Bush that will not be continued under Obama. The North American Union is fast approaching and Obama's administration will welcome it with open arms. Obama, the same as Bush, believes it is a brilliant idea to rescue the banking sector by putting the American tax payer further in the hole. Dig the bankers out of the hole and put the American people in it. What a brilliant plan! All hail Obama! Everyone is still reeling from the devilishment committed by Bush that they are giving a blind eye to Obama's treachery. Obama signed executive orders on his first day in office relating to ethics guidelines for staff members of his administration. "Transparency and the rule of law will be the touchstones of this presidency," stated Obama. However, leading up to the approval of his version of the bailout bill, the Obama administration talking heads kept telling the American public that they desperately needed Obama's stimulus package.

In the lead up to the final votes in Congress, many congressmen were told that they could not wait to have promises made by Democrats for transparency and full disclosure fulfilled. The stimulus was (like Bush's stimulus) pushed through Congress with as little deliberation and inspection as possible. The Obama administration was claiming that if Congress did not pass the bill immediately,

---

[80] Things will be worse under Obama for the simple fact that the Bush administration has paved the way for Obama's administration to take Bush's policies to the next level.

we would be facing calamitous economic consequences. After we all suffered a serious episode of *déjà-vu* (the Bush stimulus was also rushed through Congress) and Congress approved the bill for Obama to sign into law, Obama went on vacation over the long weekend; basically stating by this action that the bill could have waited.

What other important historic bills were rushed through the House and Senate without giving Congress time to debate the bill? The Federal Reserve Act of 1913, the Patriot Act, and the new stimulus packages have all been rushed through Congress—with threats attached. We were told the Patriot Act must be rammed down Congress's throat or al-Qaeda would kill us. In similar fashion, the Obama/Bush bailout bills had to pass quickly without debate or the economy would fall into the abyss. By-passing the customary debate before a bill can be agreed upon by Congress is done for the sole purpose of hiding the text of the bill from scrutiny. The more controversial aspects of those bills must be kept from the public eye. Cutting out the debate has generated questions that, so far, outnumber the answers. Do not be fooled! From the beginning, the banking lobbyists have written the bailout bills themselves. In essence, they are really bailing themselves out! On Wednesday, June 25, 2008, on Page D01, the Washington Post reported;

> *"A key provision of the housing bill now awaiting action in the Senate -- and widely touted as offering a lifeline to distressed homeowners -- was initially suggested to Congress by lobbyists for major banks facing their own huge losses from the subprime mortgage crisis, according to congressional staff members and bank officials."*
>
> *By Jeffrey H. Birnbaum*
> Washington Post Staff Writer

You do not honestly believe that President Bush and President Obama wrote these bills—do you? If you believe that Obama even read his own 1,071 page bailout, you should do what he did and go on vacation.

NEW YORK POST

24 HOURS A DAY

By BRENDAN SCOTT IN ALBANY and ANA MARIA ALAYA IN NY, AP

PRESIDENT'S DAY: President Obama and Michelle Obama exit Table Fifty-Two in Chicago last night after enjoying a Valentine's Day dinner at the eatery.

Last updated: 2:32 am
February 15, 2009
Posted: 2:17 am
February 15, 2009

After pushing Congress for weeks to hurry up and pass the massive $787 billion stimulus bill, President Obama promptly took off for a three-day holiday getaway.

Obama arrived at his home in Chicago on Friday, and treated wife Michelle to a Valentine's Day dinner downtown last night. The couple was spotted leaving upscale Table Fifty-Two, which specializes in Southern cuisine, with the first lady toting what appeared to be a doggie bag.

The president plans to spend the Presidents' Day weekend in the Windy City, and is not expected to sign the bill until Tuesday, when he travels to Denver to discuss his economic plan.

Both the House and Senate passed the bill Friday night.

The push to get the bill through before the holiday weekend was so frantic, members of Congress didn't have a chance to read all 1,071 pages of the document before they could vote.

"In a perfect world it would have been nice to have had more time to process it," said Ilan Kayatsky, a spokesman for Rep. Jerrold Nadler *(D-NY).*

Meanwhile, Gov. Paterson called yesterday for fiscal restraint with the massive influx of federal aid. His budget office estimated that New York will receive $24.6 billion over the next two years, $4 billion more than first believed. brendan.scott@nypost.com

---

Source:
http://www.nypost.com/seven/02152009/news/nationalnews/whats_the_rush__155255.htm

Notice the underlined text in the above article. What happened to Obama's hard-line stance on transparency? Obama is still saying what the people want to hear, but he is doing the exact opposite. The troops are still in Iraq,[81] and although there are alleged executive orders ready to close down Guantanamo Bay,[82] there is no mention of closing any other secret prisons that may exist.

***Source*:http://www.cnn.com/2009/POLITICS/01/21/obama.business/**

---

[81] The Obama administration has changed the pull-out of Iraq date to 2010. Originally, Obama preached a 6-month window after becoming president.

[82] The media has been reporting that closing Guantanamo Bay may be difficult.

THE FRAUD OF MONEY AND BANKING

CHAPTER VIII.

ONE WORLD CURRENCY

Coming soon to a bank near you is a single world currency. This currency will serve the vast majority of international transactions and serve as the world's primary reserve currency. The currency will no doubt serve the one world government that is now coming into view. The criminal elite are working on this now, but the collapse of the dollar must first be completed. The second phase is the introduction of the amero or the reserve currency of the American Union.[83]

Some people deny the existence of the North American Union despite the fact that they are working on it in plain view. It is similar to that old-time story about the emperor wearing no clothes. If they succeed in bringing the U.S. economy down to its knees, I surmise that by 2012 or

[83] The American Union will be the equivalent of the European Union here in the Americas. It will be spear headed by Canada, the United States, and Mexico. The reserve currency is expected to be called the Amero. All these names are subject to change at the whim of the criminal elite.

perhaps a few years therein after, they will introduce a single currency. The single currency will no doubt be similar to the Euro. Whether they name it the amero or not is yet to be determined, but it is something these criminals have mentioned.

They are also creating a union of the Gulf (or Arab) states, the African Union is forming and you will also have an Asian Union coming very soon. This is not something that is going to happen in the future; it is happening right now. *Refer* to the following links below:

African Union-
http://news.bbc.co.uk/2/hi/africa/country_profiles/3870303.stm
This article talks about how the African Union is patterned after the European Union.

The Cooperation Council for the Arab States of the Gulf -
http://english.aljazeera.net/business/2008/12/20081230153346616980.html
These are the same countries that are keeping the price of oil down in order to bankrupt the non-participating Arab countries.

The North American Community- http://www.cfr.org/publication/8102/
For now, these demons are calling it a North American Community because nosy people like me have used the term "Union." Do not be fooled, "union" and "community" echo the same concept. The predecessor of the European Union was also called "The European Economic COMMUNITY."

Forming all of these unions is essential to establishing the one world government. First, these unions must be sold to the people. Once we accept these unions, then a staged event will be engineered to have the people begging for a one world government.

On November 27, 2006, the vice president of a prominent London based investment bank recommended investors to move away from the U.S. dollar and move into the "Amero." Steve Previs, a vice president at Jefferies International Ltd., said that the amero was being developed right now. Mr. Previs stated that Canadians are "upset" and most Americans, outside of Texas, are completely unaware of the plans to replace the dollar with a North American currency.

The North American Union: Fact or Conspiracy Theory?

The Council on Foreign Relations, the Canadian Council of Chief Executives, and the Mexican Council on Foreign Relations have organized the Independent Task Force on North America. This task force advocates a greater economic and social integration among Canada, Mexico, and the United States.

In October of 2004, the task force unveiled two documents. They were:

(1). A Trinational Call for a <u>North American Economic</u> and Security Community by 2010.
(2). Building a North American Community.

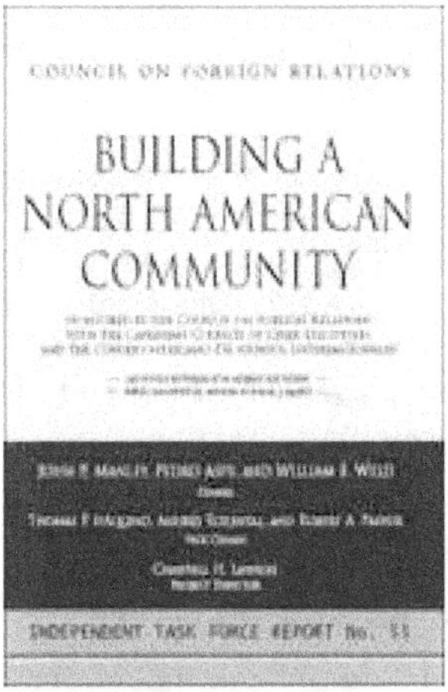

<u>Task Force Members</u>
Council on Foreign Relations Press
May 2005
175 pages
ISBN-0876093489

Psychologically deceiving is the fact that the Council on Foreign Relations sounds governmental. It is, however, nothing more than a private think tank that requires membership. These people are not voted or elected into this council by the American people. Nevertheless, they aim to get this economic union headed upward by 2010. This will happen with or without our consent. Let us take a look at some task force members and how they tie into money and banking.

Some Task Force Members and their credentials:

- **PEDRO ASPE** is CEO of Protego, a leading investment banking advisory firm in Mexico. Mr. Aspe was most recently the Secretary of the Treasury of Mexico (1988-1994). He has been a Professor of Economics at Instituto Tecnologico Autonomo de Mexico (ITAM) and has held a number of positions in the Mexican government.
- **HEIDI S. CRUZ** is an energy investment banker with Merrill Lynch in Houston, Texas. She served in the Bush White House under Dr. Condoleezza Rice as the Economic Director for the Western Hemisphere at the National Security Council, as the Director of the Latin America Office at the U.S. Treasury Department, and as Special Assistant to Ambassador Robert B. Zoellick, U.S. Trade Representative. Prior to government service, Ms. Cruz was an investment banker with J.P. Morgan in New York City.
- **NELSON W. CUNNINGHAM** is Managing Partner of Kissinger McLarty Associates, the international strategic advisory firm. He advised John Kerry's 2004 presidential campaign on international economic and foreign policy issues, and previously served in the Clinton White House as Special Adviser to the President for Western Hemisphere Affairs. He earlier served as a lawyer at the White House, as Senate Judiciary Committee General Counsel under then-chairman Joseph Biden, and as a federal prosecutor in New York.
- **THOMAS P. D'AQUINOIS** is Chief Executive of the Canadian Council of Chief Executives (CCCE), composed of one-hundred-fifty chief executives of major enterprises in Canada. A lawyer, entrepreneur, and business strategist, he has served as Special Assistant to the Prime Minister of Canada and Adjunct Professor of Law lecturing on the law of international trade. He is the Chairman of the CCCE's North American Security and Prosperity Initiative launched in 2003.
- **ALFONSO DE ANGOITA** is Executive Vice President and Chairman of the Finance Committee of Grupo Televisa, S.A. In addition, he has been a member of the Board of Directors and of the Executive Committee of the company since 1997, and served as Chief Financial Officer (1999-2003). Prior to joining Grupo Televisa, S.A., he was a partner of the law firm of Mijares, Angoitia, Cortes y Fuentes, S.C., in Mexico City.

- **LUIS DE LA CALLE PARDO** is Managing Director and founding partner at De la Calle, Madrazo, Mancera, S.C. He served as Undersecretary for International Trade Negotiations in Mexico's Ministry of the Economy and negotiated several of Mexico's bilateral free trade agreements and regional and multilateral agreements with the World Trade Organization. As Trade and NAFTA Minister at the Mexican Embassy in Washington, DC, he was instrumental in crafting and implementing the North American Free Trade Agreement.
- **WENDY K. DOBSON** is Professor and Director, Institute for International Business, Rotman School of Management, University of Toronto. She has served as President of the C.D. Howe Institute and Associate Deputy Minister of Finance in the government of Canada. She is Vice Chair of the Canadian Public Accountability Board and a nonexecutive director of several corporations.
- **RICHARD A. FALKENRATH** is Visiting Fellow at the Brookings Institution. Previously, he served as Deputy Homeland Security Adviser and Special Assistant to the President and Senior Director for Policy and Plans at the White House's Office of Homeland Security. He is also Senior Director of the Civitas Group LLC, a strategic advisory and investment services firm serving the homeland security market, a security analyst for the Cable News Network (CNN), and a member of the Business Advisory Board of Arxan Technologies.
- **CARLOS HEREDIA** is Senior Adviser on International Affairs to Governor Lazaro Cardenas-Batel of the State Michoacan. He has held senior positions in the Ministry of Finance and the Mexico City government. For over twenty years, he has worked with Mexican, Canadian, and U.S. nongovernmental organizations, promoting economic citizenship and participatory development. Since 2002, he has been Vice President of the Consejo Mexicano de Asuntos Internacionales (COMEXI).
- **CARLA A. HILLS** is Chairman and CEO of Hills & Company, an international consulting firm providing advice to U.S. businesses on investment, trade, and risk assessment issues abroad, particularly in emerging market economies. She also serves as Vice Chairman of the Council on Foreign Relations. From 1989 to 1993, Ambassador Hills served as U.S. Trade Representative in the first Bush administration, Secretary of the U.S. Department of Housing and Urban Development, and Assistant Attorney General, Civil Division, U.S. Department of Justice in the Ford administration.
- **JAMES R. JONES** is CEO of Manatt Jones Global Strategies, a business consulting firm. Formerly, he was U.S. Ambassador to Mexico (1993-97), President of Warnaco International, Chairman and Chief Executive Order of the American Stock Exchange, and U.S. Congressman from Oklahoma from 1973 to 87 (D-OK), where he was Chairman of the House Budget Committee. He was Appointments Secretary (currently known as Chief of Staff) to President Lyndon B. Johnson. He is Chairman of Meridian International and the World Affairs Councils of America, and is a board member of Anheuser-Busch, Grupo Modelo, Keyspan Energy Corporation, and the Kaiser Family Foundation.

- **LUIS RUBIO** is President of the Centro de Investigacion Para el Desarrollo-Center of Research for Development (CIDAC), an independent research institution devoted to the study of economic and political policy issues. Before joining CIDAC, in the 1970s he was Planning Director of Citibank in Mexico and served as an adviser to Mexico's Secretary of the Treasury. He is also a contributing editor of Reforma.
- **JEFFREY J. SCHOTT** is Senior Fellow at the Institute for International Economics. He was formerly an official of the U.S. Treasury and U.S. trade negotiator, and has taught at Princeton and Georgetown Universities. He has authored or coauthored fifteen books on international trade, including *NAFTA: Achievements and Challenges*, *NAFTA: An Assessment*; *North American Free Trade*, and *The Canada-United States Free Trade Agreement: The Global Impact.*

Source: http://www.cfr.org/publication/8102/

It is necessary to blow-up the U.S. dollar in order to have the American people begging for relief. The relief will come via the North American Union and the introduction of a new currency. For those who are still in denial of this, read the following Wall Street Journal publication very carefully. What methods will be used to swap Federal Reserve notes with the new currency? They will do the same things they have done in the past. They will offer you a bargain on the new currency. They will offer to trade in your dollars (fed. notes) for ameros. This is the same thing they did when they wanted to move away from hard money and introduce you to the Federal Reserve fiat. Fed agents would offer you two Federal Reserve notes for every one silver dollar. They were basically robbing the people blind.

In the early 1960s, when the price of silver jumped to over $1.29 an ounce, it was evident that further increases would make it profitable for holders of silver coins to sell them in the open market. This staged crisis[84] was the pretext to eliminate silver certificates in 1963. Hence, here we go again with another staged crisis in order to introduce another type of currency.

---

[84] All competent professional investment bankers/stock brokers know that the big banks and institutions control the markets. If you gathered the wealth of all the average household incomes in the U.S., they could still not compete with Wall St. (the institutions).

The following article can be found at the following link. http://www.marketwatch.com/News/Story/Story.aspx?guid=%7BD10536AF-F929-4AF9-AD10-250B4057A907%7D

THE WALL STREET JOURNAL. Digital Network WSJ.com

MarketWatch

TODD HARRISON

How realistic is a North American currency?

Commentary: Uniting U.S., Canada, Mexico money could result from crisis ←

By Todd Harrison

Last update: 6:12 a.m. EST Jan. 28, 2009

"World, hold on. Instead of messing with our future, open up inside." -- Bob Sinclair

NEW YORK (MarketWatch) -- Thomas Jefferson once said: "When you reach the end of your rope, tie a knot in it and hang on." As the global financial system pushes on a string, investors are desperately trying to hold tight. The New World Order is upon us, full of hope, promise and a fair amount of fear. In our recent discussion regarding the direction of our country, we noted the risks of catering to conventional wisdom and the implications for the U.S. dollar. *See MarketWatch column on New World Order.*

The Minyanville mantra is to provide financial news you need to know before you know you need it. That's a fine line to walk, as foresight often flies in the face of mainstream acceptance. In 2006, it seemed counterintuitive to forecast a "prolonged socioeconomic malaise entirely more depressing than a recession." For years, the notion of an "invisible hand" was conspiracy theory until we learned that the Working Group on Financial Markets was a central policy tool. And now, as we gaze across our historically significant horizon, we must open our minds to thoughts and ideas that may seem foreign to folks conditioned by the past and stunned by the present.

Currency crossroads

As governments take on more risk -- as they price assets on behalf of the market and transfer debt from private to public -- the common denominator, or release valve, becomes the currency. If our economic condition is allowed to take medicine in the form of debt destruction, the greenback will appreciate, and asset classes as a whole will deflate. If we continue to inject drugs that mask symptoms rather than address the disease, the likelihood of a seismic readjustment increases in kind. The deflationary forces in the marketplace are pervasive, and the "other side" of our current equation, hyperinflation, may be years away. Given the magnitude, breadth and pace of the global financial epidemic, however, we must explore each side of the twisted ride.

Years ago, the Federal Reserve wrote a "solution paper" regarding the need to combat zero-bound interest rates. The concern was the flight of capital from the U.S. and an option discussed was a two-tiered currency, one for U.S citizens and one for foreigners. Canadian economist Herbert Grubel first introduced a potential manifestation of this concept in 1999. The North American Currency -- called the "Amero" in select circles -- would effectively comingle the Canadian dollar, U.S. dollar and Mexican peso. On its face, while difficult to imagine, it makes intuitive sense. The ability to combine Canadian natural resources, American ingenuity and cheap Mexican labor would allow North America to compete better on a global stage. Experience has taught us, however, that perceived solutions introduced by policy makers and politicians don't always have the desired effect.

Did you notice the subtitle of the article? It reads; "*Uniting U.S., Canada, Mexico money could result from crisis.*" In my first book entitled, "The Conspiracy Theory Fraud,"[85] I stated:

> *"Today, there is a push to collapse the dollar and plunge the United States into a new type of depression.* ***The economy will continue to down spiral until they can introduce a new type of currency.*** *The new currency will perhaps be the amero, which will almost assuredly be followed by a cashless society."* page. 130

Why do they continue to claim that the North American Union is just conspiracy theory? As the author of the previous Wall Street Journal article eloquently stated; "*For years, the notion of an 'invisible hand' was conspiracy theory until we learned that the Working Group on Financial Markets was a central policy tool.*" The American Union is all part of that New Financial World Order they keep talking about in the media nowadays.

---

[85] The Conspiracy Theory Fraud was originally published on October 20th 2008 together with The War on Terror Fraud in an 8X10 cover. The book was titled; The Fraud of The Fraud: Have you been taken for a ride?

The New Financial World Order

Economic collapses have always been brought to the people by intelligent, well-dressed fanatics. These fanatics are hell bent on deceiving the people of the United States into accepting a one world currency. A one world currency is the key element in creating a one world government. Naturally, with a one world currency and a one world reserve bank, there will be a one world monetary system. This will be the ultimate concentration of power. Decision making will be in the hands of fewer and fewer people. In order to get your approval, they will convince the people that the only way to have a sound economy is the establishment of a New World Financial Order. It will be similar to what they did at the end of World War II with the Bretton Woods Conference.

The official name of the Bretton Woods Conference is known as the United Nations Monetary and Financial Conference. The conference was a meeting of 730 delegates from the Allied nations involved in World War II. This conference led to the set up of the International Bank for Reconstruction and Development (IBRD), the General Agreement on Tariffs and Trade (GATT), and the International Monetary Fund (IMF). This was all put in place to bankrupt the economies of the world. Only a few countries would come out victorious. Most countries that are considered to be Third World today did not have that status before the implementation of the International Monetary Fund and the World Bank. Supposedly, however, the conference was held to ensure post-war prosperity through economic cooperation. Instead, what was ensured became a new financial order.

On November 14, 2008, an economics reporter for the BBC News named Steve Schifferes states the following:

> "The meeting was part of the process led by the US to create a new international world order based on the rule of law, which also led to the creation of the United Nations and the strengthening of other international organisations."

***Source*: http://news.bbc.co.uk/2/hi/business/7725157.stm**

It is not only the U.S. economy that needs to collapse or implode. Because most countries on the planet have pegged[86] their currency to the U.S. dollar, knocking down the U.S. economy would sequentially have a domino affect around the world. You also have oil, which is measured in Federal Reserve notes (U.S. dollars). The devaluation of the dollar was the main cause for the oil price spike of 2008. The devaluation of the dollar affected oil prices in two ways. As the dollar fell against the euro and the currencies of other industrialized nations, the oil-exporting countries demanded more dollars per barrel of oil to protect their ability to meet expenses paid in foreign currencies. When oil prices were trading at their highest peak in 2008, the euro was able to purchase oil at about three times less the cost it would with dollars. Countries that were pegged to the dollar paid for high oil prices because of the weakness of the dollar and an increased oil demand from China and India.

For these reasons, if the United States collapses, so will the global financial infrastructure. The criminal elite have this knowledge. The world economy must collapse in order to get the public to ask the bankers to fix the economy with a new financial order.[87] This is why the Prime Minister of England is asking for a new Bretton Woods Conference.

---

[86] Refer to the section on "Pegging" found on p. 115

[87] A new financial order and the term a new world order can be used interchangeably. They are parts of the same agenda.

Telegraph.co.uk

Gordon Brown's Bretton Woods summit call risks spat with Nicholas Sarkozy

Gordon Brown's call for a summit to re-write the rules of global capitalism has left him vying with French President Nicholas Sarkozy to be Europe's dominant leader.

By James Kirkup and Bruno Waterfield in Brussels
Last Updated: 10:14AM BST 17 Oct 2008

Angela Merkel, Nicolas Sarkozy, Gordon Brown, and Francois Fillon met recently at an emergency meeting at the Elysee Palace in Paris Photo: Reuters

The Prime Minister on Wednesday called for a "new Bretton Woods", an overhaul of the world economic order that has stood since 1944. Mr. Brown says the major summit is justified by the need to establish new rules to prevent a repeat of the recent world financial crisis.

He made the call at a meeting of European leaders in Brussels, where he has been feted by some leaders in the wake of Britain's widely-emulated banking bail-out this week.

However, Mr Sarkozy holds the presidency of the EU and with it the right to speak for the bloc on the world stage. The French President made his own call for a "new Bretton Woods" earlier this month, arguing that it was time to replace the "Anglo-Saxon" model of unrestrained markets has failed.

Diplomats in Brussels said that Mr Brown had technically breached EU protocol by appearing to assume a leadership role for himself. The Prime Minister wants dozens of world leaders to meet for a major one-off summit where they would rewrite the rules of international capitalism that have stood since 1944.

The foundations of the current world financial and economic system were laid at Bretton Woods in New Hampshire in 1944. Led by Franklin D Roosevelt, Western leaders created the International Monetary Fund, the World Bank and laid down common standards for open markets around the world.

Calling for "very large and very radical changes", Mr Brown said he was seeking nothing less than "a new Bretton Woods". Speaking at a summit of European Union leaders in Brussels, Mr Brown said the recent crisis proved the need for much more international co-operation on the regulation of banks and other financial institutions.

He said: "We now have global financial markets, global corporations, global financial flows. But what we do not have is anything other than national and regional regulation and supervision." The Prime Minister has won considerable international credit for his £37 billion recapitalization of Britain's banks, a measure that has been followed by both US and European leaders.

He now wants to use that political capital to create a new system of international financial regulation, led by a reformed and ***enlarged*** *IMF. "We need a global way of supervising our financial system," he said. As the first step, Mr. Brown revealed that 30 of the world's biggest banks will now be supervised by what amount to global regulators.*

The banks, understood to include RBS, Deutsche Bank and Credit Suisse, will each be overseen by a "college of supervision" taking in regulatory officials from each of the countries in which they operate. In a paper circulated among EU leaders, Mr Brown proposed a range of other reforms, including: New rules to curb bankers' bonuses and salaries, stopping pay schemes that "encourage excessive and irresponsible risk-taking". Common rules to make banks disclose their assets and liabilities, to prevent them hiding "toxic" loans.

A crackdown on the "shadow banking system" of hedge funds and other financial institutions that trade complex financial products often based on debt. "There is now a general agreement there should be an international leaders' meeting," Mr Brown said. He added that the summit could be held in November or December, and signalled he wants the new US president - whether that is Barack Obama or John McCain - to attend.

The meeting should go "beyond the Group of Eight" rich nations and take in countries like South Africa, Brazil, India and China, Mr Brown said.

The summit should agree common international rules for financial regulation, cross-border supervision of multinational firms and a "global early warning system" to watch for future financial crises. It should also try to agree a new world trade deal, he said. The Prime Minister has been proposing international financial reform for several years but has failed to win support. Aides say he sees the recent crisis an opportunity to advance his agenda.

Once a virtual pariah in Brussels for his dismissive attitude towards his EU colleagues, Mr Brown this week finds himself feted as the virtual economic saviour of the continent. Reflecting his new status, several European leaders were quick to back his call for a summit. Angela Merkel, the German Chancellor, backed Mr Brown's call, saying it was time to "rethink the world's financial system and prevent any repetition" of the current crisis. Despite his recent successes, Labour remains well behind the Conservatives in the polls, putting Mr Brown on course to be out of a job at the next general election.

Some British diplomats speculate that Mr Brown might aspire to take on the leadership of a reformed IMF or some other leading post in a new financial regime. Mr Brown ducked a question asking if he had any aspirations for a new job in the new "financial and regulatory architecture" he says he wants to construct.

Smiling broadly, he replied only: "I am not an architect."

***Source*:**
http://www.telegraph.co.uk/news/worldnews/europe/france/3205033/Gordon-Browns-Bretton-Woods-summit-call-risks-spat-with-Nicholas-Sarkozy.html

In an interview that Henry Kissinger[88] made with the financial news channel CNBC, he basically stated that the Obama administration should use the world crisis to bring in a "New World Order." Kissinger repeated this notion in an article he wrote for the International Herald Tribune. This is reminiscent of Kissinger's CFR colleague Gary Hart—who made a similar suggestion to the Bush administration after the 9/11 Terror Attacks. (Refer to The War on Terror Fraud)

Henry Kissinger is as demonic and criminal as they come. It is fitting that he was born in Bavaria, Germany. This is the accepted birth place of the Illuminati. In 1955, he joined the Council on Foreign Relations as the Study Director in Nuclear Weapons and Foreign Policy. This media darling is a product of the Rockefeller family and had advised baby Bush on the attacks of Iraq and Afghanistan. Kissinger has dodged many law suits, including one filed on September 10, 2001. The suit was filed by the family of General René Schneider, a former Commander-in-Chief of the Chilean Army. The lawsuit made claims that Kissinger ordered the assassination of General Schneider for the general's refusal to participate in the overthrow of the Chilean Government.

***Sources*: http://www.guardian.co.uk/world/2001/sep/12/2**
http://www.youtube.com/watch?v=Ugt_TVu05nk

Henry Kissinger

---

[88] Henry Alfred Kissinger was the 56th Secretary of State of the United States from 1973 to 1977. He continued to hold the position of Assistant to the President for National Security Affairs, which he first assumed in 1969 until 1975.

INTERNATIONAL
Herald Tribune
THE GLOBAL EDITION OF THE NEW YORK TIMES

The chance for a new world order

By Henry A. Kissinger
Published: January 12, 2009

As the new U.S. administration prepares to take office amid grave financial and international crises, it may seem counterintuitive to argue that the very unsettled nature of the international system generates a unique opportunity for creative diplomacy. That opportunity involves a seeming contradiction. On one level, the financial collapse represents a major blow to the standing of the United States. While American political judgments have often proved controversial, the American prescription for a world financial order has generally been unchallenged. Now disillusionment with the United States' management of it is widespread.

At the same time, the magnitude of the debacle makes it impossible for the rest of the world to shelter any longer behind American predominance or American failings. Every country will have to reassess its own contribution to the prevailing crisis. Each will seek to make itself independent, to the greatest possible degree, of the conditions that produced the collapse; at the same time, each will be obliged to face the reality that its dilemmas can be mastered only by common action.

Even the most affluent countries will confront shrinking resources. Each will have to redefine its national priorities. An international order will emerge if a system of compatible priorities comes into being. It will fragment disastrously if the various priorities cannot be reconciled. The nadir of the existing international financial system coincides with simultaneous political crises around the globe. Never have so many transformations occurred at the same time in so many different parts of the world and been made globally accessible via instantaneous communication. The alternative to a new international order is chaos.

The financial and political crises are, in fact, closely related partly because, during the period of economic exuberance, a gap had opened up between the economic and the political organization of the world. The economic world has been globalized. Its institutions have a global reach and have operated by maxims that assumed a self-regulating global market.

The financial collapse exposed the mirage. It made evident the absence of global institutions to cushion the shock and to reverse the trend. Inevitably, when the affected publics turned to their national political institutions, these were driven principally by domestic politics, not considerations of world order. Every major country has attempted to solve its immediate problems essentially on its own and to defer common action to a later, less crisis-driven point. So-called rescue packages have emerged on a piecemeal national basis, generally by substituting seemingly unlimited governmental credit for the domestic credit that produced the debacle in the first place - so far without more than stemming incipient panic.

International order will not come about either in the political or economic field until there emerge general rules toward which countries can orient themselves. In the end, the political and economic systems can be harmonized in only one of two ways: by creating an international political regulatory system with the same reach as that of the economic world; or by shrinking the economic units to a size manageable by existing political structures, which is likely to lead to a new mercantilism, perhaps of regional units.

A new Bretton Woods-kind of global agreement is by far the preferable outcome. America's role in this enterprise will be decisive. Paradoxically, American influence will be great in proportion to the modesty in our conduct; we need to modify the righteousness that has characterized too many American attitudes, especially since the collapse of the Soviet Union.

That seminal event and the subsequent period of nearly uninterrupted global growth induced too many to equate world order with the acceptance of American designs, including our domestic preferences. The result was a certain inherent unilateralism - the standard complaint of European critics - or else an insistent kind of consultation by which nations were invited to prove their fitness to enter the international system by conforming to American prescriptions.

Not since the inauguration of President John F. Kennedy half a century ago has a new administration come into office with such a reservoir of expectations. It is unprecedented that all the principal actors on the world stage are avowing their desire to undertake the transformations imposed on them by the world crisis in collaboration with the United States. The extraordinary impact of the president-elect on the imagination of humanity is an important element in shaping a new world order. But it defines an opportunity, not a policy.

The ultimate challenge is to shape the common concern of most countries and all major ones regarding the economic crisis, together with a common fear of jihadist terrorism, into a common strategy reinforced by the realization that the new issues like proliferation, energy and climate change permit no national or regional solution.

***Source*: http://www.iht.com/articles/2009/01/12/opinion/edkissinger.php**

The Bretton Woods Agreements

How can anyone begin to express the fraud of the World Bank and the International Monetary Fund? Let us begin with the history of these international organizations. In 1944, soon after World War II ended, delegates from 44[89] countries checked into the Sprawling Mount Washington Hotel for the United Nations Monetary and Financial Conference. The goal was to set up a system of rules, institutions, and procedures that would regulate the international monetary system. Most of the conference was dominated by the United States and England. This was all according to the plan established on the infamous Atlantic Charter.

The Atlantic Charter was a secret meeting between Winston Churchill and President Franklin D. Roosevelt on August 9, 1941. The meeting took place in a chartered flight to Newfoundland. The two men returned on the 12th of August. Two days later they officially announced the meeting took place. Three months after that announcement, the arranged attack on Pearl Harbor took place. The attack swung public opinion and allowed the United States to enter the war on the side of England and its allies. Deals were made and the stage was set for a post-war international monetary system negotiated by the United States

---

[89] In numerology, the number 44 is a powerful number. Numerologists believe the number 4 vibrates with paying attention to detail and building a solid foundation for the future. The numbers eleven (11), twenty-two (22), thirty-three (33) and forty-four (44) are the four master numbers in numerology. The master number 44 is also considered to be an important number by the alchemists. They believe that people who are born under this number have the ability to create magic around themselves and others. Now you have (Obama) the 44th president, reportedly born on the 4th day of the 8th month (8=two 4s) who won the U.S. presidential election on the 4th day of November of 08' with a 44 year old wife. Coincidence? Perhaps....

and England. It was a simple replay of the famous *Treaty of Versailles* after World War I, which was primarily negotiated by the United States, England, and France. There was no participation by the war's losers. This is why New York (Wall St.) and London (Lombard St.)[90] are the financial capitals of the world. The Bretton Woods Conference established the United States currency as the world's reserve currency. All participating countries would peg their currency to the U.S. dollar. In return, the United States promised to peg the U.S. dollar to a fixed rate of $35 per ounce of gold.

By 1968, the attempt to defend the dollar at a fixed peg of $35/ounce began to fizzle. The fizzle was a result of the burden that the Vietnam War was putting on the U.S. dollar. The infusion of billions of dollars over flooded the currency exchange markets with U.S. dollars. This caused a devaluation of the dollar (which was pegged to gold). By the time the Vietnam War reached 1970, the United States entered its first ever trade deficit. This caused the Nixon administration to take drastic measures. Among those measures was a 90-day wage and price control, a discontinuation of a 10% import tax (surcharge), and discontinuation of the direct conversion of dollars into gold (except on the open market). These actions by the Nixon administration are commonly referred to by historians as *The Nixon Shock*.

Location: PLACENTIA BAY Newfoundland, Canada
Date: 08/9/41 - 8/12/41
Code Name: RIVIERA
Main Participants: Roosevelt, Churchill
Major Decisions: Agreement on war aims. Atlantic Charter.

[90] Lombard St. was a piece of land granted by King Edward I to goldsmiths from the Lombardy region of Italy.

By February of 1973, the Bretton Woods currency exchange markets had closed and were reopened a month later as a floating currency regime. Nowadays, the bankers are licking their chops at the possibility of finally perfecting their international monetary programs. Many of the programs they are going to introduce were on the table at the Bretton Woods Conference but were not implemented.

A single currency and a world central bank were being proposed by the father of *Keynesian Economics*, John Maynard Keynes. His one world currency was to be called the *Bancor*. The currency was allegedly going to be fixed to thirty commodities, gold included. The aim was to stabilize the average prices of commodities and the currency itself as the main medium of exchange and store of value. Most of these ideas failed to appeal to the nations of the world because globalism was in its infancy.

John Maynard Keynes, 1883-1946.

THE FRAUD OF MONEY AND BANKING

CHAPTER IX.

THE OCCULT AND THE SYMBOLIC MEANING OF MONEY

Many people contend that the symbols found on most of our institutions today have nothing to do with secret societies. However, when you research and read what some of the authorities on those societies have to say about these symbols, they always have a meaning. The U.S. dollar bill is especially laced with symbolism. Nevertheless, it is almost impossible to have an intelligent discussion about those symbols with people who have no knowledge of secret societies, or those who are low-level members of those societies.

There is no question that most symbols are open to many interpretations. Still, there are some historical insights and other direct connections that can explain some symbols that we see on a day to day basis. For instance, the principals of money are deeply rooted in the principals of electricity and the flow of water. This is why money is also referred to as currency. But what is a current, and what does it have to do with money? Let us examine this.

The Flow of Water

It is a well established fact that the original bankers were merchants. The word "merchant" comes from the Middle English *march (e) ant*, which comes from the Latin *mercari*. The word "*mare*" or "*maris*" translates as the "sea" in Latin. In the Spanish language (a dialect of Latin) the word for "sea" is "*mar.*" The second part of the word *mercari* is "*cari.*" This is the same word that has been drafted into the words car, carriage, and cargo. The etymology from the Spanish is *cargo*, "burden" from *cargar* "to load, impose taxes," from Late Latin *carricare*, "to load on a cart," from Latin *carrus*, "wagon." The ancient bankers heavily relied on the currents to allow their ships to transport their products (merchandise). These ancient merchants (bankers) can be traced back to the Phoenicio-Canaanite civilization, which was an enterprising maritime trading culture that spread across the Mediterranean between the period of 1550 BC to about 300 BC—before spreading to Greece, Rome, and eventually Western Europe. These early merchants were in business because of the water currents that took their ships to the desired trading post. In those days most merchants traveled on a river. The currency of a river is directed by its banks. River banks are found on both sides of a river and they direct the flow of the currency. Therefore, a river bank works to control the current. This is the same thing they did in order to stagnate the economies of the world. They set up banks to redirect the flow of the currency (money) or the cash flow.

In finance, when there is an abundance of M1 or physical money in the economy, it is referred to as liquidity. Liquidity is also the ability to convert an asset into cash quickly. When the Federal Reserve cuts interest rates, it is also known as "pumping liquidity into the market." These are not merely interesting analogies. The criminal elite are very symbol oriented. For example, since ancient times, the sun and the moon have been symbolized by gold and silver. The eight phases of the moon represent the four quarters that represent the whole dollar. During most of the seventeenth and eighteenth centuries, the Spanish dollar coin was the de facto national currency of the American colonies. When change was needed in a business transaction, the dollar was essentially cut into eight pieces or "bits." Thus came the term "pieces of eight" from these early times and "two bits" from our time. Two bits equaled twenty-five cents. Ultimately, if you have four quarters, you have eight bits.

Make no mistake about it; one of the main purposes of the current monetary system is to extract revenue from you as chattel property. It is a major way for them to sustain slavery. As stated in *Volume One: The Conspiracy Theory Fraud,* you have to be invited to participate in your own enslavement. The main principal of this fraud deals with the elements of water and electricity. Obviously water creates life and all things that live are electrical. They have a certain amount of electrical current moving through them. The foods we eat and fluids we drink contain mineral salts that form electrolytes after they dissolve in the fluids (waters) of our bodies. They are present in our blood, urine, the fluid inside our body's cells, and the fluid in the space surrounding the cells. Sodium, calcium, chloride, magnesium, and potassium are the most common electrolytes in the human body. They are essential for many heart, nerve, and muscle functions. They also play an important role in keeping fluid levels normal in different body compartments.

As you might have already guessed from their name, electrolytes are electrically charged, which means that they can conduct electrical impulses. The body needs electrical impulses to make muscle cells contract. The generation of an electrical impulse by a cell requires an electrical voltage to be maintained across the membrane of that cell. The differences in electrolyte levels create and maintain these electrical voltages.

***Refer to*: http://www.medicinenet.com/electrolytes/article.htm**

It is all symbolism based on the ancient occults[91] that the elites keep hidden from the people. For instance (keeping with the same example), electricity is a secondary energy source. In other words, we get it from the conversion of other sources of energy such as coal, natural gas, oil, nuclear power, and other natural resources called "primary sources." The primary sources of money have always been gold and silver. Their energies are symbols of the moon and the sun. The alchemical[92] symbol for the moon is silver and the alchemical symbol for the sun is gold. When you look at the moon, it gets its light from the sun. The moon sheds no light of its own. The sun, symbolic of the gold, becomes the primary source of money. The energy of the moon and the sun allow life to exist on the planet.

When you understand the symbolism of the Unknowns, you will understand the deceptions used to maintain the enslavement. A slave cannot be maintained for long periods of time because it is against nature. Therefore, the slave must be invited to participate in the slave masters reality. The reality is set-up to stop your waters. The flow of water on the planet is symbolic to the flow of water in man. This correlates in the sense that both man and earth are composed of 75% to 80% water. When that water flows free, it feeds the fish, the wildlife, and nourishes the land. To prevent that water from flowing free and natural, you build a dam or a river bank. This allows you to

---

[91] The word "occult" comes from the Latin word *occultus* and is commonly defined as; Secret, disclosed, or communicated only to the initiated. Also, hidden from view.

[92] Alchemy (Arabic: الخيميـــاء *al-kimia*) is an occultic practice. It attempts to achieve the supreme wisdom and immortality using and making many substances described as having supernatural properties. Alchemy is partly credited with originating the basic principals of inorganic chemistry concerning procedures and the identification of many current substances. Alchemy dates back several thousand years and can be found in the great empires of old in a complex network of philosophical schools.

regulate the flow (current). What would happen to the people and the animals that depended on that free flowing current? Those people will now be subject to poverty, pestilence, and disease. What happens to the price of that land? It can then be bought for pennies on the dollar. This is what has happened to most countries on the planet. The criminal elite are regulating the flow (currency, money) in order to stagnate our waters (economies).

The criminal elite that run the United States are selling the country's infrastructure to both foreign and domestic corporations. Private corporations now own the roads, the prisons, and the water supply of our municipalities. There is no federal or state constitution on American soil that permits government to do such things.

This would also apply to the banker bailout bill. A foundation called Freedom Works[93] claims it plans to file a lawsuit against the banker bailout bill. The chairman, Mr. Dick Armey, who is the former Republican House majority leader, distributed a memorandum to Congress stating, "When Congress delegates so much authority to the executive branch with so few rules to guide its discretion, Congress unconstitutionally transfers its lawmaking power to the executive." President Obama's economic proposal is to create a so-called "bad bank" that will be ran by the FDIC. This bank would buy troubled mortgage-backed securities that are stagnating on Wall Streets books. Again, President Obama is keeping up with the Bushes'. His $787 billion package (in reality about $1.53 trillion) is nothing more than legislaturing the United States into a complete socialistic country (we are not far from that now).

On Wall Street, talk of the nationalization of banks like Citigroup Inc., and Bank of America Corp., has investtors worried that the government will take control and wipe out shareholders in the process. On February 20, 2009, White House Press Secretary Robert Gibbs stated, "This administration continues to strongly believe that a privately

[93] The FreedomWorks Institution was founded in 1984. It is a conservative non-profit organization based in Washington D.C. The institutions goal is to reduce the size of government, and lower taxes.

held banking system is the correct way to go, ensuring that they are regulated sufficiently by this government." As we have seen, Obama's administration is run by the bankers themselves. There is no line dividing the government and the banking elite. Obama's banker bill, which passed the House by a 246 to183 vote, was written for the benefit of the bankers. It is 1,071-pages of first class garbage. What citizen is going to sit down and read a 1,071 page book? It is the same as reading the entire Holy Bible! How long would that take?

In the interest of being informed, I have read as much as I could (at my leisure). From my readings of the bill, I surmise that the bill will further subvert our economy with private projects, expanded government, and an unchecked spending spree that is deceptively being regarded as a stimulus package. It is all done to stagnate your flow. They have subdued the economy in an attempt to stave off the great awakening that is currently taking place. As the Piscean age[94] comes to an end, more and more people are beginning to recognize that something is very wrong in our society. As the criminal elite continue to push their agenda, they anticipate that the people will be too hungry and too broke to worry about what the elites are doing.

---

[94] There are many different dates given to the end of the age of Pisces. It takes about 25,920 years for a complete cycle of the precession of the equinoxes. There are at least two theories about how long great ages last. Some believe that the twelve great ages each last an equal amount of time, about 2,160 years. Others believe that the lengths of the great ages are irregular. They believe that a great age lasts as long as the vernal equinoctial point remains within the boundary of that particular constellation. According to that theory, the Age of Pisces would last longer than the Age of Aquarius because the constellation of Pisces takes up more real estate on the ecliptic path than the constellation of Aquarius.

The Symbols of The Seal of the United States Treasury Department

The original Seal of the Department of the Treasury, designed in 1778. The Latin inscription is an abbreviation for the phrase Thesauri Americae Septentrionalis Sigillum, which means "The Seal of the Treasury of North America." The seal was simplified in 1968 and now bears the words "The Department of the Treasury" and the date of the Department's establishment, 1789.

The symbol of the United States Treasury Department was created by Francis Hopkins, a judge of the Admiralty Court of Pennsylvania. Admiralty law is commonly referred to as maritime law. Again, the first syllable of the word maritime is *mar,* which means the seas or the ocean. Maritime law is a code of laws that regulate maritime offenses. It is a body of private international laws to govern the relationships between private corporations that operate vessels on the waters.

Hopkins made claims that he was responsible for the design of the first official flag of the United States. He also influenced the design of the Great Seal of the United States that is currently seen on the back of the one dollar bill. Although the creation of the seal is credited to William Barton, Hopkins' influence appears in the design of the unfinished pyramid with the All-Seeing Eye. The pyramid was originally used by Hopkins in a design he helped create for a continental $50 note issued in 1779.

The emblem on the front shows a thirteen-stepped pyramid, with the motto: "Perennis" (Everlasting). The nature print on the back depicts three arrows.

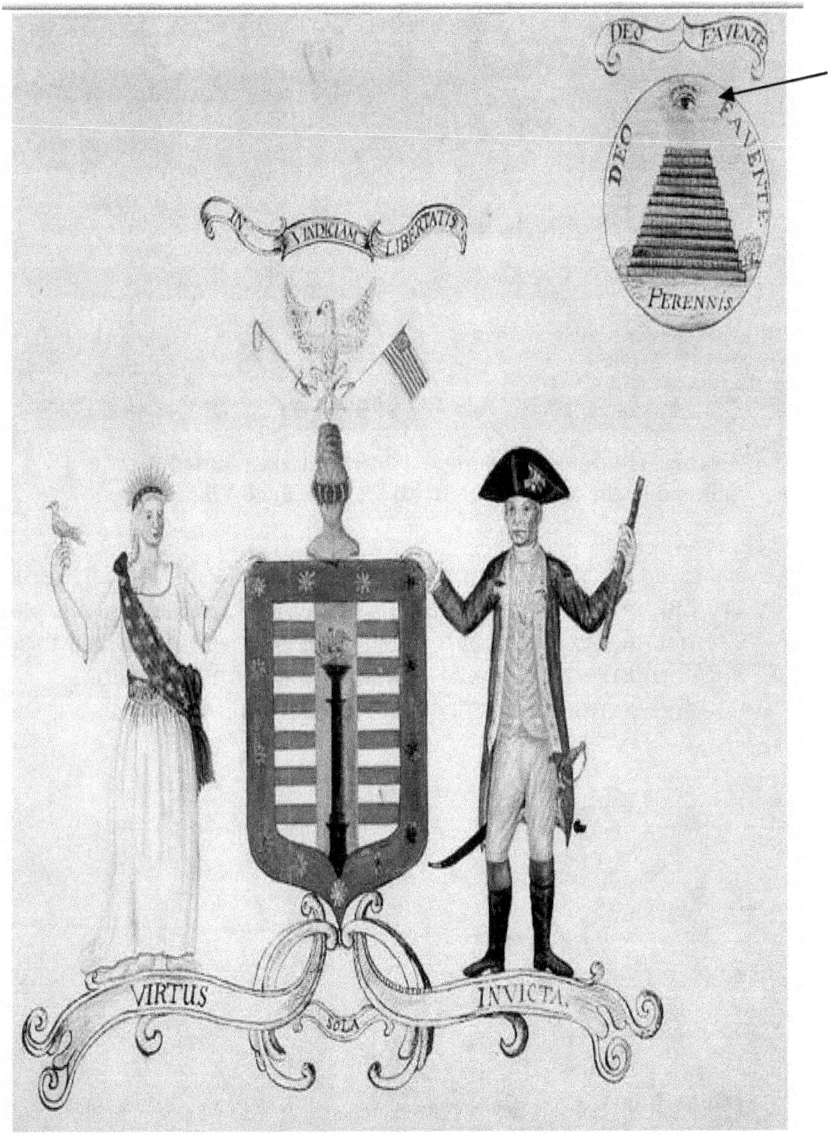

William Barton's design for the reverse of the Great Seal, in 1782 appears in the upper right. This was the original reverse seal of the United States.

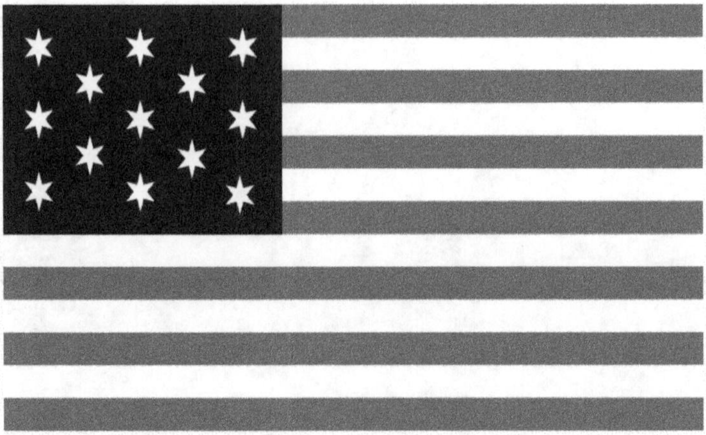

Francis Hopkins flag design. Notice the six-pointed stars are aligned in the form of the British Union Jack Flag.

The symbols that appear on the seal of the Treasury Department are: a scale, a key, a shield, and 13 hexagram stars on a chevron symbol. Two chevron symbols superimposed on each other in different directions give you the compass and the square symbol of freemasonry.

This shield displaying two superimposed chevrons are from Bolligen, a municipality in the Bern administrative district of the canton of Bern, Switzerland.

The Compass & the Square of Freemasonry

The word *chevron* is usually used in reference to a badge or insignia used in military or police uniforms. The chevron symbol usually indicates rank or length of service, or heraldry.[95] Keep in mind that the Knights Templar were said to have originally been a military order of warrior monks out of France. The Templars were to protect Christian pilgrims on their way to and from the holy land. Thus, they symbolized protection like the roof of a house (also shaped like a chevron). *See below*

The origin of the word "chevron" comes from Middle English *cheveron*, from Old French *chevron*, meaning a rafter[96] (from the meeting of rafters at an angle).

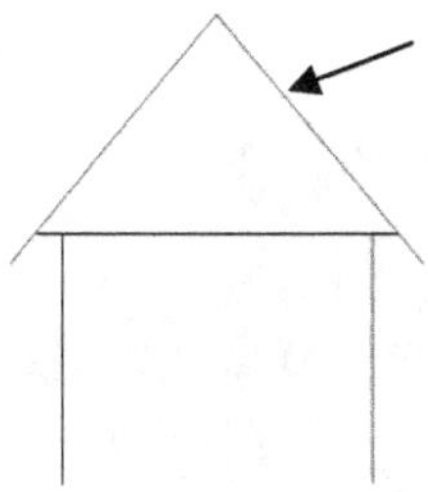

Hence, the Knights Templar were known as *chevalier,*[97] which is the French word for "horseman." The term was also used as a title. In Spanish they were known as *caballeros*, but in English the title would be "knight."

Notice how the same exact chevron symbol, minus the thirteen stars (the compass replaces stars), appears in the coat of arms of the United Grand Lodge of England.

---

[95] Heraldry is the practice of designing, displaying, describing, and recording coats of arms and badges.

[96] A rafter is defined as the framing member directly supporting the roof sheathing. A rafter usually follows the angle of the roof and may be a part of a roof truss.

[97] By the phonetics alone, one may conclude that the words chevron and chevalier are closely related and share in the same root. In the Spanish language, the term "caballeros" is also related.

The United Grand Lodge of England is the main governing body of Freemasonry within England and Wales and in some countries, predominantly ex-British Empire and Commonwealth countries outside the United Kingdom. It is the oldest Grand Lodge in the world, deriving its origin from 1717. Together with the Grand Lodge of Ireland and the Grand Lodge of Scotland, It is considered to be the home Grand Lodge of Freemasonry.

The chevron symbol shows only one 90° angle of the square. An angle of 90°degrees is a right ang le. Why is it referred to as a right angle? If you look at a square, there is a left side and a right side. Yet, all the angles on that square are called right angles. The word "right" supplants the word "correct." It is the only angle which is right (correct) for stones that will form a wall, a building, a cathedral, synagogue, or mosque. Any other angle is masonically incorrect. The symbolism of the square is nothing obscure. Operative Stonemasons use it to prove the Perfect Ashlars.[98] If the stone fits the square, it is ready for the builders use. Hence, the universal significance of the word "square" means moral, upright, honorable, and dealing fairly with others.

As for the balancing scales, they are a symbol of justice. Libra is the seventh sign of the zodiac and it is sometimes referred to as *The balance*. Libra also starts on the seventh month called *Septem* in Latin. Obviously, according to our current calendar, September is recognized as the ninth month. However, it was changed from the calendar of the ancients. In the ancient Middle East, the beginning of the year was March.

March- one	September- Septimo
April- Two	October- Octavo
May- Three	November- Noveno
June- Four	December- Decimo
July- Five	
August- Six	

[98] A Perfect Ashlar is a stone that is "squared" or ready for construction. In freemasonry, it represents perfection or an upright man who is virtuous and filled with piety. Such a man can only be judged by nature.

The sun enters (Septem) Libra around the time of year when day and night are of equal length. Symbolically, the light of god and the darkness of evil are equal or the same. When we think of justice, we think of something that is good or positive for our society. However, the evenly balanced scale represents an equal balance of good and evil in society. The criminal elites' mentality is such that, if there is an over flowing abundance of good in society, evil must be created in order to balance it with the good. If there is too much evil, then the inverse must happen in order to balance with the evil. The original glyph or symbol for Libra is said to represent the setting sun when it appears to be halfway down or equal to the dark. The original glyph or symbol for Libra looks like the following:

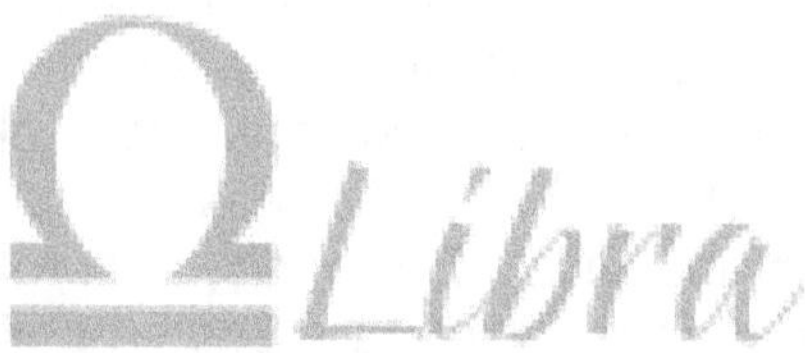

In some cultures, this glyph is said to symbolize the setting Sun as it descends over the horizon.

The standard image of the astrological sign of Libra is that of the scales, indicative of balance and equilibrium. It is a sign of cosmic reciprocity meant to be in cooperation rather than in competition. The origin of the word Libra derives from the Latin meaning "balances" or "scales." Often, a statue of the Goddess of Justice holding the scales or balances is erected over the domes of modern court houses. Most courthouses in the United States and England have images of Lady Justice. Lady Justice typically adorns a long robe and a blindfold. She either holds the balancing scales, or is depicted with the scales in close proximity around her.

This statue of Lady Justice is located above the Hill Street entrance of the Los Angeles County Courthouse at Hill and 1st Street.

The key found in the seal of the U.S. Treasury Department is said to represent the Treasury Departments authority. Coincidentally, the key is one of the most important symbols of freemasonry. In ancient secret societies, the key was usually symbolic of silence. In the ritual of the Master's Degree of the Adonhiramite Rite,[99] there is the following catechism:

> Q: What do you conceal?
> A: All the secrets which have been entrusted to me.
> Q: Where do you conceal them?
> A: In the heart.
> Q: Have you a key to gain entrance there?
> A: Yes, Right Worshipful.
> Q: Where do you keep it?
> A: In a box of coral which opens and shuts only with ivory teeth.
> Q: Of what metal is it composed?
> A: Of none. It is a tongue obedient to reason, which knows only how to speak well of those of whom it speaks in their absence as in their presence.

---

[99] Adonhiram means "the lord Hiram" or exalted master; from the Hebrew Adon and from the Greek Adonis. The name is given to Hiram Abif, known in freemasonry as King Solomon's Chief Architect.

The key represents secrecy. It also represents the secret passwords. In the lower degrees of freemasonry, the key has been replaced with the modern symbol of the "instructive tongue." The key, however, is still recognized as a symbol for secrecy in the Royal Arch Degrees. The key serves as a reminder to the initiated that they must lock-up or conceal the secrets. Even today, when people promise to keep a secret, they jokingly may say, "I am locking up my lips and throwing away the key." Certainly most people do not have any idea where these terms and ideas came from.

In the Bible, Jesus tells Peter, "I will give unto thee the keys of the kingdom of heaven." *Refer to the book of Matthew 19:16.* The keys that Jesus is referring to in this passage are the secrets of heaven. Jesus, himself, belonged to several secret societies, such as the Order of the Essences and the Order of Melchisedek.

When the disciples asked Jesus why he spoke to the people in parables, Jesus answered:

The Book of Matthew 13:11

"Because it is given unto you to know the mysteries of the kingdom of heaven, but to them it is not given."

(King James Version)

"The knowledge of the secrets of the kingdom of heaven has been given to you, but not to them."

(New International Version)

"To you it has been granted to know the mysteries of the kingdom of heaven, but to them it has not been granted."

(New American Standard Bible)

"To you it has been given to know the secrets of the kingdom of heaven, but to them it has not been given."

(English Standard Version)

"To YOU it is granted to understand the sacred secrets of the kingdom of the heavens, but to those people it is not granted."

(The New World Translation: Jehovah's Witness)

The head of the United States Treasury Department is the Secretary of the Treasury. The current law found at *31 U.S.C. § 301* reads as follows (in part):

> *(a) The Department of the Treasury is an executive department of the United States Government at the seat of the Government.*
>
> *(b) The head of the Department is the Secretary of the Treasury.The Secretary is appointed by the President, by and with the advice and consent of the Senate.*

The word secretary comes from the word "secret." It has its origin in the Latin word *secernere*, "to distinguish" or "to set apart," the passive participle[100] *secretum*, meaning "having been set apart," with the eventual connotation of something private or confidential. A *secretarius* was a person,

[100] A participle is a verbal adjective: a form of the verb that acts like an adjective. There are four participles in Latin: the present active, the perfect passive, the future active, and the future passive.

therefore, overseeing government or business confidentially. The job was usually done for a powerful individual, such as a king, emperor, or religious leader.

Understanding the criminal elite's usage of words and terms are the key to unlocking their mystery. The money kept by the Department of the Treasury is not to be kept secret from the public. This is simple. The money collected by the Treasury Department belongs to the people. They do not have the authority to keep their expenditures a secret. What secrets behold the U.S. Treasury Department? Why is the key used on their seal? What does a key have to do with money? It all goes back to the Knights Templar. The Knights Templar basically shaped today's monetary systems. As the goldsmiths of the Middle Ages, they created the idea of fractional reserve banking.

Rosicrucianism was derived from the Knights Templar and exists today as part of some of the orders in freemasonry. For instance, the Adonhiramite Rite of freemasonry consists of twelve degrees.

1st Degree— Apprentice
2nd Degree— Fellow Craft
3rd Degree— Master Mason
4th Degree— Perfect Master
5th Degree— Elect of Nine
6th Degree— Elect of Perignan
7th Degree— Elect of Fifteen
8th Degree— Minor Architect
9th Degree— Grand Architect
10th Degree— Scottish Master
11th Degree— Knight of the Sword, Knight of the East, or of the Eagle.
12th Degree— Knight of Rose Croix.

The twelfth degree is of the Knights of the Rose Croix. The Rose Croix Degree is also the 18th Degree of the Ancient and Accepted Scottish Rites. When you say *Rose Croix*, it is the same as saying "the Rose and Cross" which is the same as "*Rosicruci*" or Rosicrucian. These are some of the people who have set up our current economic structure.

In 1693, King Louis XIV of France set up the *Ordre Royal et Militaire de Saint-Louis* (The Royal and Military Order of Saint Louis).

The Order had three classes:

- *Grand-Croix* (Grand Cross)
- *Commandeur* (Commander)
- *Chevalier* (Knight)

Officers of the order included, after the grand master, a *Trésorier* (Treasurer), a *Greffier* (Registrar) and a *Huissier* (Gentleman Usher). This appears to be almost the same hierarchy of the U.S. Treasury Department. Also, notice the arch[101] found in a city named after King Louis IX of France (Reign, 1226 AD – 1270 AD), also known as St. Louis.

The City of St. Louis in the state of Missouri

[101] The arch in the picture is said to be a symbol of the Royal Arch Degree of freemasonry. It is located on the historic riverfront of St. Louis near the Gateway Arch. Because of the historical significance of the church, it was left intact while the neighboring buildings were all torn down to make way for the Gateway Arch. The Old Courthouse sits at the heart of the city of Saint Louis, with the arch to the east, near the rivers edge.

The winged angels are called cherubs. Also notice the *Ark of the Covenant* atop the coat of arms. The Ark of the Covenant is of Egyptian origin. The "Eye of Providence" represents the eye of the Egyptian god Horus. This is where we get the word "Horizon", the sun rising.

This is an apron worn by Masons of the Royal Arch degree.[102] Notice the All-Seeing Eye of Providence, the wings forming an arch and the chevron symbol facing in the same direction as it does in the seal of the U.S. Treasury Department. Usually, the compass is pointing upward and the chevron is pointing downward.

The Holy Royal Arch Degree is a York Rite degree of freemasonry. The York Rite Degrees are not numbered like the more widely publicized Scottish Rite Degrees. But sequentially, the Holy Royal Arch would be the 7th York Rite Degree. This Degree marks the half-way point to the culmination of the York Rite Order of the Temple Degree or Knights Templar Degree.

Many people who are against religion or against the Vatican believe that the Knights Templar are a benevolent group. They believe this because of the continuous war between the two groups. They do not understand that this is a war between the Old World Order (religion) and the New World Order (the bankers). Neither side is fighting on your behalf. Understand that you are the prize. Who ever wins gets to rule you. The religious elites had been ruling for thousands of years. Their refusal to relinquish power to the New World Order has caused the ongoing war against the bankers.

---

[102] The Royal Arch Degree catechism asks, *"Are you a Royal Arch Mason?"* To which the reply is made, *"I - AM - THAT - I - AM."* This is what the god of Israel told Moses his name was in the book of Exodus 3:14. The term has been translated as "Jehovah." In freemasonry, the term "I am that I am" basically means; what you see is what you get; nothing more, nothing less.

The symbols of the UNITED STATES $Dollar Bill

The U.S. dollar bill is the most talked about paper money on the planet. It is also the most used and most recognizable piece of paper. It is made of 75% cotton and 25% linen. The paper also contains red and blue fibers of various lengths that are evenly distributed throughout its surface. The current dollar bill that we hold today was designed under the Franklin D. Roosevelt administration. Although there was not much change made to the front of the dollar bill, the back was revamped.

Many have come to believe that the reverse seal of the United States is a Masonic symbol. However that is not exactly correct. The symbol was only borrowed or passed down to freemasonry by the older secret societies. Some high ranking Freemasons, such as BRENT MORRIS 33° Grand Cross, Supreme Council 33°, Ancient Accepted Scottish Rite USA, author of *complete idiots guide to Freemasonry*, New York: Penguin Publishing, and managing editor of the largest-circulation Masonic magazine in the world, called the *Scottish Rite Journal,* has made claims that "The eye in the pyramid is not nor has ever been a Masonic symbol."

Refer to: http://www.calodges.org/no406/ALLCEYE.HTM

Later on in the same article, Mr. Morris concludes the following:

> "It's hard to know what leads some to see Masonic conspiracies behind world events, but once that hypothesis is accepted, any jot and tittle can be misinterpreted as "evidence." The Great Seal of the United States is a classic example of such a misinterpretation,

and some Masons are as guilty of the exaggeration as many anti-Masons.

The Great Seal and Masonic symbolism grew out of the same cultural milieu. While the all-seeing eye had been popularized in Masonic designs of the late eighteenth century, it did not achieve any sort of official recognition until Webb's 1797 Monitor. Whatever status the symbol may have had during the design of the Great Seal, it was not adopted or approved or endorsed by any Grand Lodge. The seal's Eye of Providence and the Mason's All-Seeing Eye each express Divine Omnipotence, but they are parallel uses of a shared icon, not a single symbol."

Although I agree that the All-Seeing Eye is not of Masonic origin, it was introduced into Freemasonry by sinister secret societies under the cloak of philosophy and revolution. The orders of the Illuminati were big on philosophy. Many of the great philosophers and free thinkers during the French Revolution were Illuminati members. However, the Illuminati did not originate in France. It is a well established fact that the earliest traces of the Illuminati are found in Germany under Adam Weishaupt. On the following page there is a picture of the eye inside the pyramid. This symbol is found on the oldest cathedral in Northern Europe. The Aachen Cathedral, frequently referred to as The Imperial Cathedral (in German: *Kaiserdom)*, is a Roman Catholic Church in Aachen, Western Germany. The church is known as the Royal Church of St. Mary and it dates as far back as the Middle Ages.

The Aachen Cathedral- ***Here you have the pyramid and the eye on a site that pre-dates the introduction of the United States seal found on the back of the dollar bill.***

This 1914 French-Indian Freemasonic Symbol is identical to the reverse seal found in back of the U.S. dollar bill. Notice the date of 1914. This is twenty years before it was placed on the U.S. dollar in 1935.

On November 26, 1958, a non-profit, non-political organization was founded in Pondicherry (currently known as Puducherry), India called, The New World Union. This doctrine mirrors the doctrine established by the Illuminati during the French Revolution in a host of articles known as, *The Declaration of the Rights of Man and Citizen.* The last article of *The Declaration of the Rights of Man and Citizen* was adopted on August 27, 1789 by the National Constituent Assembly (*Assemblée nationale constituante*), during the period of the French Revolution. This was to be the ground work for establishing the French Constitution. The symbol or iconography of *The Declaration of the Rights of Man and Citizen* has the Illuminati symbol depicting the eye inside the pyramid. The French used this symbol publicly in 1788 and again in 1793, when a new *Declaration of the Rights of Man and Citizen* was written by a commission that included Louis Antoine Léon de Saint-Just (commonly known as Saint-Just) and Marie-Jean Hérault de Séchelles. These men were members of the *Committee of Public Safety* and were heavily involved in the "Reign of Terror" during the period of the French Revolution. (Refer to Volume Two: *The War on Terror Fraud*)

The Great Seal of the United States was first used publicly in 1782. Two different continents using the same icons! Is there a connection here?

From Hunt's *History of the Seal of the United States.*

Notice the Eye and the Pyramid. Also notice the resemblance to the many depictions of the Ten Commandments

This is the 1793 version of the declaration. Notice that the eye sits on top of a pyramid shaped hat. The eye is already inside a pyramid.

The following is according to the Department of the Treasury's own website.

Question – What is the significance of the symbols on the back of the one-dollar bill? I'm particularly interested in the eye and the pyramid.

Answer – The eye and the pyramid shown on the reverse side of the one-dollar bill are in the Great Seal of the United States. The Great Seal was first used on the reverse of the one-dollar Federal Reserve note in 1935. The Department of State is the official keeper of the Seal. They believe that the most accurate explanation of a pyramid on the Great Seal is that it symbolizes strength and durability. The unfinished pyramid means that the United States will always grow, improve and build. In addition, the "All-Seeing Eye" located above the pyramid suggests the importance of divine guidance in favor of the American cause. The inscription ANNUIT COEPTIS translates as "He (God) has favored our undertakings," and refers to the many instances of Divine Providence during our Government's formation. In addition, the inscription NOVUS ORDO SECLORUM translates as "A new order of the ages," and signifies a new American era.

***Source*: http://www.treas.gov/education/faq/currency/portraits.shtml#q1**

The underlined sentence above clearly states that they only believe these explanations are the most accurate. However, they are not sure. How could the official keeper of the seal, the Department of the State, not know its exact meaning without a shadow of a doubt? The truth of the matter is that they know the answer. They simply cannot tell you. As stated in Volume One: *The Conspiracy Theory Fraud*, they always have two meanings for words and symbols. They have one meaning for you, and one meaning for them. The meanings of these symbols, as stated in the Treasury Departments website, make little to no sense at all. The only plausible symbolic meaning is that of the pyramid representing durability. This symbol makes some sense because the pyramids at the Giza Plateau are over 10,500 years old.[103] However, the All-Seeing Eye has nothing to do with guidance. The All-Seeing Eye was used by the ancients to describe the gods, also referred to as, "the Watchers."

> "The Watchers were "a specific race of divine beings known in Hebrew as nun resh 'ayin, *'irin'* (resh 'ayin, *'ir'* in singular), meaning 'those who watch' or 'those who are awake', which is translated into Greek as Egrhgoroi *egregoris* or *grigori*, meaning 'watchers'. These Watchers feature in the main within the pages of pseudepigraphal and apocryphal works of Jewish origin, such as the *Book of Enoch* and the Book of Jubilees. Their progeny, according to Hebrew tradition, are named as *nephilim*, a Hebrew word meaning 'those who have fallen' or 'the fallen ones', translated into Greek as gigantez, *gigantes*, or 'giants' - a monstrous race featured in the Theogony of the hellenic writer Hesiod (c. 907 BC)."

Source - Andrew Collins, *From the Ashes of Angels - The Forbidden Legacy of a Fallen Race* (1996) p. 3

One of the most respected and quoted Freemasons of all time, Albert G. Mackey 33°, wrote the following in:

---

[103] The history books generally point to 2560 BC as the approximate date the pyramid of Khufu was under construction. There is however, no concrete evidence to prove that the Giza Plateau was built during this era. These monuments at the Giza Plateau line up with various stars as they appeared in the sky in the Age of Leo, circa 12,500 years ago, possibly before the last Ice Age. On the first day of spring, in the years surrounding 10,500 BC, the Sphinx (a Lion) faced in the direction of the constellation of Leo (also a Lion), as it rose with the sun at dawn on the Vernal Equinox. The Pyramids themselves are also aligned with Orion's Belt only as it appeared in the sky during that same point in time.

THE ENCYCLOPAEDIA [ENCYCLOPEDIA] OF FREEMASONRY AND ITS KINDRED SCIENCES *Copyright*, 1873 and 1878, by *Moss & Co*. and A.G. Mackey.

All-Seeing Eye. An important symbol of the Supreme Being, borrowed by the Freemasons from the nations of antiquity.

(continued)
On the same principle, the open eye was selected as the symbol of Divine watchfulness and care of the universe.

p.47

According to some Freemasonic scholars, freemasonry is traced back to the building of King Solomon's Temple in Jerusalem circa 967 BC. King Solomon is considered to be one of the wisest kings in Hebrew history. In the Bible, according to the Book of Proverbs, King Solomon concurred with the doctrine of the eye as being watchful.

Proverbs 15:3

> "The eyes of the LORD are in every place, beholding the evil and the good."

-King James Version

Next we have the Latin phrase, NOVUS ORDO SECLORUM, which is on the Treasury's website as meaning, "A new order of the ages," signifying "A new American era." Many argue that this does not translate as "A new world order." They argue that such a translation would be *Novus Ordo Mundi.* Although this is true, it does not mean that "Novus Ordo Seclorum" cannot translate the same. The etymology of the word *secular* is from Middle English, from Anglo-French *seculer,* from Late Latin *saecularis,* from *saeculum*, meaning, "the present world," from Latin, generation, age, century, and world; akin to the Welsh word *hoedl*, meaning lifetime. The term "world" is not the actual physical planet. It is the state of the planet or the state of the current era or period of any given time. Often times people confuse the end of the world with the end of an era (age). Many believe that the year 2000 brought in the new era of the Aquarian age. Others believe the new age will begin in the year 2012. Either way, the Aquarian Age will mark the end of the Piscean Age. Hence, it will mark the end of the world (age, era). The preachers and teachers who claim Jesus spoke about the end of the planet (world) do not now what they are talking about. But they are not supposed to know.

Matthew 24:3

"And as he sat upon the Mount of Olives, the disciples came unto him privately, saying; tell us, when shall these things be? And what shall be the sign of thy coming, and of the end of the world?"

-King James Version

The Greek word for world in this verse is "*aion.*" It is defined as:

1. For ever, an unbroken age, perpetuity of time, eternity.
2. The worlds, universe
3. Period of time, age

***Source*: http://net.bible.org/strong.php?id=165**

A good question to ask is, "why does the phrase *NOVUS ORDO SECLORUM* appear in a 1914 French-Indian Masonic publication?" (*Refer to page 206*). With all the history regarding the Illuminati capturing France, why would something like this be ignored?

Here is the same exact phrase found on the coat of arms of the Yale School of Management, which is the graduate business school of Yale University (an Illuminati front).

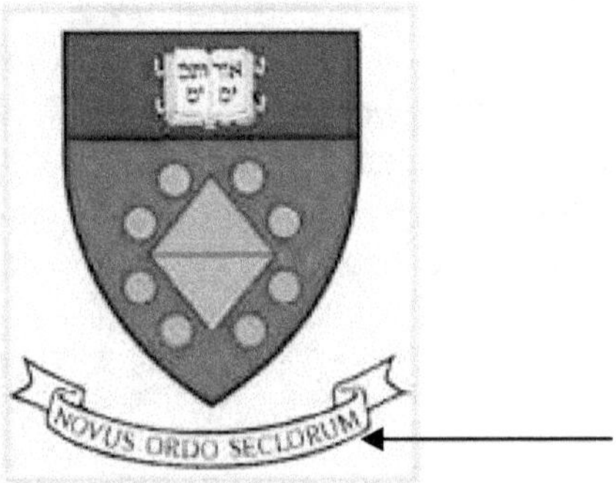

The school was established in 1976, two-hundred years removed from 1776. Keep in mind, 1776 is the year Adam Weishaupt established the Bavarian Illuminati Order. The Roman Numerals on the bottom of the pyramid on the reverse seal reads 1776. Isn't it strange that the phrase "Novus Ordo Seclorum" appears on our money and on this financial institution of learning? How about the fact that it was founded by a Skull and Bones member?

In 1976, Skull & Bones member William H. Donaldson, founder of *Donaldson, Lufkin & Jenrette* and former Chairman of the Securities and Exchange Commission (as appointed by fellow Bonesman, baby Bush), founded the school as *The Yale School of Organization and Management*. The funds to establish the school materialized when Frederick William Beinecke, a Yale College alumnus, left $15 million dollars to Yale University in 1971. This university has produced some of the top criminal elites of the United States. The university was founded by James Pierpont, who was a great-great relative of John Pierpont Morgan (JP Morgan). JP Morgan was once considered the most important banker in the United States.

After the founder James Pierpont died, the school took on the surname of its benefactor, Elihu Yale. The University was funded with opium drug money obtained by Elihu Yale, who was very a successful businessman from Wales.[104] He made a fortune while living in India as a representative of the infamous *British East India Company.*

CBS NEWS

Skull And Bones

Secret Yale Society Includes America's Power Elite

June 13, 2004 | by Rebecca Leung

(in part)

Skull and Bones, with all its ritual and macabre relics, was founded in 1832 ***as a new world version of secret student societies that were common in Germany*** *at the time. Since then, it has chosen or "tapped" only 15 senior students a year who become patriarchs when they graduate -- lifetime members of the ultimate old boys' club. (continued)*

---

[104] Although the school was not founded by Elihu Yale, he became the benefactor (as the main investor of the school) when the real founder James Pierpont died in 1714.

President Bush has tapped five fellow Bonesmen to join his administration. Most recently, he selected ***William Donaldson****, Skull and Bones 1953, the head of the Securities and Exchange Commission. Like the President, he's taken the Bones oath of silence.*

Read the complete article at:
http://www.cbsnews.com/stories/2003/10/02/60minutes/main576332.shtml

It is a well accepted fact that Skull & Bones is of German origin. It is also a well accepted fact that the Illuminati order was first established in Germany by Adam Weishaupt. Why do these people, who are not supposed to be connected to the people who created the symbols on the dollar bill, continue showing up with the same exact symbols in their doctrines?

Before I close, it is important that the reader understand that she must join in this war against the criminal elite and their unknown masters. You may start by getting out of debt. Stop using their credit cards and instruments of debt. Understand that there is not a bank or corporation on the face of the earth that has your best interest at heart. Their only interest is to maintain the slavery.

-Outro-

In 1968, the son-in-law of President Franklin Delano Roosevelt, Curtis B. Dall, wrote a book from close personal experience concerning the famous four-time president entitled, *My Exploited Father-in-Law.* I would like to close this volume with what he wrote in the dedications of that book.

"Dedicated to young Americans—May you benefit from observing how certain shadowy forces contrive to ruthlessly advance their own financial and ideological objectives at your expense. They select, then groom, and ultimately control many of our highest government officials. They plan the wars and through "foreign policy" arrange to set the stage for incidents to initiate hostilities. They overwork the word "Peace" to mislead you and create a plausible smoke screen in order to conceal their real operations. You can recognize who "they" are.

Hence, I say, young Americans, be alerted-be more effective than my unsuspecting and bemused generation.. Sally-forth, defend and preserve for yourself and those who follow you our great heritage of freedom and liberty."

-Curtis B. Dall

"THE FIRST TEMPRATURE"

APPENDIX A

Andrew Jackson Bank Veto Message, July 10, 1832

The present corporate body, denominated the president, directors, and company of the Bank of the United States, will have existed at the time this act is intended to take effect twenty years. It enjoys an exclusive privilege of banking under the authority of the General Government, a monopoly of its favor and support, and, as a necessary consequence, almost a monopoly of the foreign and domestic exchange. The powers, privileges, and favors bestowed upon it in the original charter, by increasing the value of the stock far above its par value, operated as a gratuity of many millions to the stockholders....

The act before me proposes another gratuity to the holders of the same stock, and in many cases to the same men, of at least seven millions more....It is not our own citizens only who are to receive the bounty of our Government. More than eight millions of the stock of this bank are held by foreigners. By this act the American Republic proposes virtually to make them a present of some millions of dollars.

Every monopoly and all exclusive privileges are granted at the expense of the public, which ought to receive a fair equivalent. The many millions which this act proposes to bestow on the stockholders of the existing bank must come directly or indirectly out of the earnings of the American people....

It appears that more than a fourth part of the stock is held by foreigners and the residue is held by a few hundred of our own citizens, chiefly of the richest class.

Is there no danger to our liberty and independence in a bank that in its nature has so little to bind it to our country? The president of the bank has told us that most of the State banks exist by its forbearance. Should its influence become concentered, as it may under the operation of such an act as this, in the hands of a self-elected directory whose interests are identified with those of the foreign stockholders, will there not be cause to tremble for the purity of our elections in peace and for the independence of our country in war? Their power would be great whenever they might choose to exert it; but if this monopoly were regularly renewed every fifteen or twenty years on terms proposed by themselves, they might seldom in peace put forth their strength to influence elections or control the affairs of the nation. But if any private citizen or public functionary should interpose to curtail its powers or prevent a renewal of its privileges, it can not be doubted that he would be made to feel its influence.

It is to be regretted that the rich and powerful too often bend the acts of government to their selfish purposes. Distinctions in society will always exist under every just government. Equality of talents, of education, or of wealth can not be produced by human institutions. In the full enjoyment of the gifts of Heaven and the fruits of superior industry, economy, and virtue, every man is equally entitled to protection by law; but when the laws undertake to add to these natural and just advantages artificial distinctions, to grant titles, gratuities, and exclusive privileges, to make the rich richer and the potent more powerful, the humble members of society the farmers, mechanics, and laborers who have neither the time nor the means of securing like favors to themselves, have a right to complain of the injustice of their Government. There are no necessary evils in government. Its evils exist only in its abuses. If it would confine itself to equal protection, and, as Heaven does its rains, shower its favors alike on the high and the low, the rich and the poor, it would be an unqualified blessing. In the act before me there seems to be a wide and unnecessary departure from these just principles.

Nor is our Government to be maintained or our Union preserved by invasions of the rights and powers of the several States. In thus attempting to make our General Government strong we make it weak. Its true strength consists in leaving individuals and States as much as possible to themselves in making itself felt, not in its power, but in its beneficence; not in its control, but in its protection; not in binding the States more closely to the center, but leaving each to move unobstructed in its proper orbit.

Experience should teach us wisdom. Most of the difficulties our Government now encounters and most of the dangers which impend over our Union have sprung from an abandonment of the legitimate objects of Government by our national legislation, and the adoption of such principles as are embodied in this act. Many of our rich men have not been content with equal protection and equal benefits, but have besought us to make them richer by act of Congress. By attempting to gratify their desires we have in the results of our legislation arrayed section against section, interest against interest, and man against man, in a fearful commotion which threatens to shake the foundations of our Union. It is time to pause in our career to review our principles, and if possible revive that devoted patriotism and spirit of compromise which distinguished the sages of the Revolution and the fathers of our Union. If we can not at once, in justice to interests vested under improvident legislation, make our Government what it ought to be, we can at least take a stand against all new grants of monopolies and exclusive privileges, against any prostitution of our Government to the advancement of the few at the expense of the many, and in favor of compromise and gradual reform in our code of laws and system of political economy....

APPENDIX B

Federal Reserve Act (in parts….)

Section 1. Short Title and Definitions

Article 1

Short Title *
Be it enacted by the Senate and House of Representatives of the United States of America in Congress assembled, That the short title of this Act shall be the "Federal Reserve Act."

Article 2

Definition of "Bank"
Wherever the word "bank" is used in this Act, the word shall be held to include State bank, banking association, and trust company, except where national banks or Federal reserve banks are specifically referred to. For purposes of this Act, a State bank includes any bank which is operating under the Code of Law for the District of Columbia.

Article 3

Definitions of Other Terms
The terms "national bank" and "national banking association" used in this Act shall be held to be synonymous and interchangeable. The term "member bank" shall be held to mean any national bank, State bank, or bank or trust company which has become a member of one of the reserve banks created by this Act. The term "board" shall be held to mean Board of Governors of the Federal Reserve System; the term "district" shall be held to mean Federal reserve district; the term "reserve bank" shall be held to mean Federal reserve bank; the term "the continental United States" means the States of the United States and the District of Columbia.

Article 4

Definition of "Bonds and Notes of the United States"
The terms "bonds and notes of the United States," "bonds and notes of the Government of the United States," and "bonds or notes of the United States" used in this Act shall be held to include certificates of indebtedness and Treasury bills issued under section 3104 of title 31.

Section 2. Federal Reserve Districts

Article 3

....every national banking association in the United States is hereby required, and every eligible bank in the United States and every trust company within the District of Columbia, is hereby authorized to signify in writing, within sixty days after the passage of this Act, its acceptance of the terms and provisions hereof
....every national banking association within that district shall be required within thirty days after notice from the organization committee, to subscribe to the capital stock of such Federal reserve bank in a sum equal to six per centum of the paid-up capital stock and surplus of such bank, one-sixth of the subscription to be payable on call of the organization committee or of the Board of Governors of the Federal Reserve System, one-sixth within three months and one-sixth within six months thereafter, and the remainder of the subscription, or any part thereof, shall be subject to call when deemed necessary by the Board of Governors of the Federal Reserve System, said payments to be in gold or gold certificates.

Article 9

No individual, copartnership, or corporation other than a member bank of its district shall be permitted to subscribe for or to hold at any time more than $25,000 par value of stock in any Federal reserve bank. Such stock shall be known as public stock and may be transferred on the books of the Federal reserve bank by the chairman of the board of directors of such bank.

Section 2B. Appearances Before and Reports to the Congress

(a) Appearances before the Congress

1. The Chairman of the Board shall appear before the Congress at semi-annual hearings, as specified in paragraph (2), regarding
   A. the efforts, activities, objectives and plans of the Board and the Federal Open Market Committee with respect to the conduct of monetary policy; and
   B. economic developments and prospects for the future described in the report required in subsection (b).
2. The Chairman of the Board shall appear
   A. before the Committee on Banking and Financial Services of the House of Representatives on or about February 20 of even numbered calendar years and on or about July 20 of odd numbered calendar years;
   B. before the Committee on Banking, Housing, and Urban Affairs of the Senate on or about July 20 of even numbered calendar years and on or about February 20 of odd numbered calendar years; and
   C. before either Committee referred to in subparagraph (A) or (B), upon request, following the scheduled appearance of the Chairman before the other Committee under subparagraph (A) or (B).

(b) Congressional report. The Board shall, concurrent with each semi-annual hearing required by this section, submit a written report to the Committee on Banking, Housing, and Urban Affairs of the Senate and the Committee on Banking and Financial

Services of the House of Representatives, containing a discussion of the conduct of monetary policy and economic developments and prospects for the future, taking into account past and prospective developments in employment, unemployment, production, investment, real income, productivity, exchange rates, international trade and payments, and prices.

Section 7. Division of Earnings

Dividends and Surplus Fund of Reserve Banks
(a)

1.
    A. After all necessary expenses of a Federal reserve bank have been paid or provided for, the stockholders of the bank shall be entitled to receive an annual dividend of 6 percent on paid-in capital stock.
    B. The entitlement to dividends under subparagraph (A) shall be cumulative.
2. That portion of net earnings of each Federal reserve bank which remains after dividend claims under subparagraph (1)(A) have been fully met shall be deposited in the surplus fund of the bank.

(b) Transfer for fiscal year 2000.

1. The Federal reserve banks shall transfer from the surplus funds of such banks to the Board of Governors of the Federal Reserve System for transfer to the Secretary of the Treasury for deposit in the general fund of the Treasury, a total amount of $3,752,000,000 in fiscal year 2000.
2. Of the total amount required to be paid by the Federal reserve banks under paragraph (1) for fiscal year 2000, the Board shall determine the amount each such bank shall pay in such fiscal year.

3. During fiscal year 2000, no Federal reserve bank may replenish such bank's surplus fund by the amount of any transfer by such bank under paragraph (1).

Use of Earnings Transferred to the Treasury

(b) The net earnings derived by the United States from Federal reserve banks shall, in the discretion of the Secretary, be used to supplement the gold reserve held against outstanding United States notes, or shall be applied to the reduction of the outstanding bonded indebtedness of the United States under regulations to be prescribed by the Secretary of the Treasury. Should a Federal reserve bank be dissolved or go into liquidation, any surplus remaining, after the payment of all debts, dividend requirements as hereinbefore provided, and the par value of the stock, shall be paid to and become the property of the United States and shall be similarly applied.

Section 25A. Banking Corporations Authorized to Do Foreign Banking Business*

Article 11

Citizenship of Stockholders

Except as otherwise provided in this section, a majority of the shares of the capital stock of any such corporation shall at all times be held and owned by citizens of the United States, by corporations the controlling interest in which is owned by citizens of the United States, chartered under the laws of the United States or of a State of the United States, or by firms or companies, the controlling interest in which is owned by citizens of the United States.

The complete Federal Reserve Act can be read at:
http://www.federalreserve.gov/aboutthefed/fract.htm

APPENDIX C

Congressman Brad Sherman's Statement on Bailout Passage

October 3, 2008

Washington, D.C. **-** Today, Congress approved the $700 billion Wall Street Bailout Bill. Under the Bill, hundreds of billions of dollars will be used to buy toxic assets currently in safes in London, Shanghai, and Riyadh, Saudi Arabia. Bailed out Wall Street firms will use their bail out money to pay *million dollars a month salaries,* and to even increase them to two million dollars a month. (For details, see paper at BradSherman.house.gov.)

Our economy will not do well in the months to come, and dropping $700 billion on Wall Street is *not* going to make things much better. But now Wall Street will use the same fear mongering tactics which were used to pass the Bill, in order to justify the bill.

In order to pass the Bill, Wall Street declared that unless they received $700 billion in unmarked bills, the Dow would drop by 4,000 points and blood would flow in the streets. The passage of the Bill will have little positive economic effect, and the fall and winter will be bad times for our economy. But in the coming weeks, Wall Street will justify the Bill by saying that we averted those very same calamities they had predicted during their successful effort to create panic, and pass the Bill.
The worst abuses of the Bill can be minimized if Congress, and especially the press, begins an unprecedented level of ferocious oversight:

- We have to make sure that Paulson spends the money and the orderly rate of less than $50 billion month (as he has promised), not at a frantic pace that spends it all by January 20th, 2009.

- We have to make sure that Paulson treats all financial entities fairly, whether they be firms he likes, or firms he doesn't like. (It will take incredible investigative journalism to see whether the executives of any bailed-out firms are making secret contributions to Section 527 organizations, which are responsible for a big chunk of today's political advertising).
- When a firm receives a billion dollars in bail-out cash, we must report on which of its executives are receiving that cash in the form of salaries in excess of $1 million a year. (The bill allows unlimited salaries to be paid by bailed-out firms, and does not contain a provision preventing the bail-out cash from being used to pay those salaries.)
- Each time a U.S.-headquartered entity sells billions of toxic assets to the Treasury, we must ask whether that U.S. entity is just acting as an intermediary. We must ask whether those toxic assets were in foreign safes on September 20th, 2008. We must be aware of the China two-step (described in a paper at BradSherman.house.gov), in which a foreign investor who made bad business decisions can sell toxic assets to a U.S. entity on Monday, and Paulson can buy those toxic assets with taxpayer dollars on Tuesday.

No one will ever be able to prove that the Bailout Bill helped or hurt our economy during the coming fall and winter. **Only two things are certain: the bill will provide hundreds of billions of dollars to investors who made bad decisions and Wall Street executives; and our children and grandchildren will now face a national debt that is hundreds of billions of dollars higher.**

APPENDIX D

The President's Private Sector Survey (PPSS), commonly known as "THE GRACE COMMISSION"

January 12, 1984

The Honorable Ronald Reagan
President of the United States
The White House
Washington, D.C.

Dear Mr. President,

Following your directive to identify and suggest remedies for waste and abuse in the Federal Government, the President's Private Sector Survey (PPSS) offers recommendations which would save:

$424 billion in three years, rising to

$1.9 trillion per year(by the year 2000.

These proposals would transform the Federal debt situation as follows:

	Federal Debt ($ trillions)		*Annual Interest on Federal Debt ($ billions)*	
	Without PPSS	With PPSS	Without PPSS	With PPSS
1990	$ 3.2	$2.0	$ 252.3	$89.2
1995	6.2	2.2	540.9	62.3
2000	13.0	2.5	1,520.7	75.1

You asked the American people to help you get the Government "off their backs." If the American people realized how rapidly Federal Government spending is likely to grow under existing legislated programs, I am convinced they would compel their elected representatives to "get the Government off their backs." In our survey to search out ways to cut costs in the Government, great emphasis was placed on the spending outlook, which is as follows:

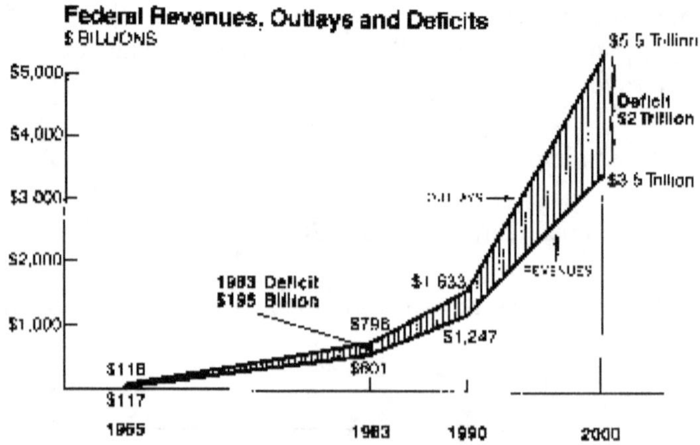

If fundamental changes are not made in Federal spending, as compared with the fiscal 1983 deficit of $195 billion, a deficit of over ten times that amount, $2 trillion, is projected for the year

2000, only 17 years from now. In that year, the Federal debt would be $13.0 trillion ($160,000 per current taxpayer) and the interest alone on the debt would be $1.5 trillion per year ($18,500 per year per current taxpayer).

Mr. President, these projections are the result of a joint effort between PPSS and a leading U.S. economic forecasting firm. They are the result of very careful study and drove us to seek out every possible savings opportunity, a "like tireless bloodhounds," as you requested.

In the course of the search by our 36 Task Forces, chaired by 161 top executives from around the country and staffed by over 2,000 volunteers that they provided, we came up with 2,478 separate, distinct, and specific recommendations which are the basis for the carefully projected savings. For practical purposes, these savings, if fully implemented, could virtually eliminate the reported deficit by the 1990's versus an alternative deficit of $10.2 trillion in the decade of the 1990's if no action is taken.

Equally important, the 2,478 cost-cutting, revenue-enhancing recommendations we have made can be achieved without raising taxes, without weakening America's needed defense build-up, and without in any way harming necessary social welfare programs.

Because we are starting from a deficit of $195 billion, every dollar we can stop spending is a dollar that the Government does not have to borrow. With future Government borrowing costs at 11 percent (versus 10.75 percent now and 14.5 percent when you took office) and inflation taken at 6 percent per year over the longer run, these savings compound quickly.

Applying these interest and inflation rates, the result is that a dollar saved today accumulates to $32 over 12 years and $71 over 17 years. Thus, any potential saving made, as compared to not making the saving, translates into a difference in cumulative spending of 32 times that amount through 1995 and 71 times that amount through the end of the century.

Therefore, $100 billion in reduced Government spending in year one equates cumulatively to $7.1 trillion in the year 2000. And since borrowings are decreased by this amount, so will the national debt decrease.

This is, of course, a horrendous prospect. If the American people understood the gravity of the outlook, they would not, I believe, support representatives who might let it happen.

Mr. President, you have been so correct in resisting attempts to balance the budget by increasing taxes. The tax load on the average American family is already at counterproductive levels with the underground economy having now grown to an estimated $500 billion per year, costing about $100 billion in lost Federal tax revenues per year.

The size of the underground economy is understandable when one considers that median family income taxes have increased from $9 in 1948 to $2,218 in 1983, or by 246 times. This is runaway taxation at its worst.

Importantly, any meaningful increases in taxes from personal income would have to come from lower and middle income families, as 90 percent of all personal taxable income is generated below the taxable income level of $35,000.

Further, there isn't much more that can be extracted from high income brackets. If the Government took 100 percent of all taxable income beyond the $75,000 tax bracket not already taxed, it would get only $17 billion, and this confiscation, which would destroy productive enterprise, would only be sufficient to run the Government for seven days.

Resistance to additional income taxes would be even more widespread if people were aware that:

One-third of all their taxes is consumed by waste and inefficiency in the Federal Government as we identified in our survey. Another one-third of all their taxes escapes collection from others as the underground economy blossoms in direct proportion to tax increases and places even more pressure on law abiding taxpayers, promoting still more underground economy-a vicious cycle that must be broken.

With two-thirds of everyone's personal income taxes wasted or not collected, 100 percent of what is collected is absorbed solely by interest on the Federal debt and by Federal Government contributions to transfer payments. In other words, all individual income tax revenues are gone before one nickel is spent on the services which taxpayers expect from their Government.

AUTHORS NOTE: The above paragraph is the most important writing and discovery of this commission's findings.

Our survey studied the small as well as the major items of cost savings, items of broad national impact as well as those of a more localized nature. I believe you will be interested in a few random examples of what we found:

In the Northwest, the Federal Power Marketing Administration is selling subsidized power at one-third of market rates. If the Federal power were priced at market, there would be a three-year increase in revenues of $4.5 billion, which equates to the three-year personal income taxes of 676,000 median income American families who are thus subsidizing a discrete group in one part of the country.

The Civil Service and Military Retirement Systems provide to participants three times and six times the benefits, respectively, of the best private sector plans. The Government's civilian and military employees retire at an earlier age, typically age 55 and 40, respectively, versus 63 to 64 in the private sector, with substantially more liberal benefit formulas than their private sector counterparts. In addition, the pensions of Federal retirees are fully indexed for inflation-a rarity in the private sector. Modifying major Federal pensions to provide benefits comparable to those of the best private sector plans, slightly better in the case of military pensions, would result in three-year savings of $60.9 billion, equivalent to the three-year income taxes of 9.2 million median income families.

A relatively small item in the overall, but representative of many, is the prohibition of competitive bidding on the movement of military personnel household goods to and from Alaska and Hawaii, despite a DOD test showing that competitive bidding would reduce costs by as much as 26 percent. Elimination of this provision would save $69.5 million in three years, equivalent to the three-year income taxes of 10,400 median income families.

We found Congressional interference to be a major problem. For example, because Congress obstructs the closing of bases that the military wants to close, the three-year waste is $367 million. In total, PPSS recommends three-year savings of $3.1 billion by closing excess military bases, equivalent to the three-year income taxes of 466,000 median income families.

Mr. President, these are just a few of the absurd situations that we found throughout the Government that add up to billions of dollars per year and where the opportunities for savings are clearly available.

Some of the recommendations made by PPSS have been made before. Others are entirely new. Regardless of their origins, the focus must now be on implementation. The current economic trends are simply too serious to delay action any longer.

PPSS has submitted 36 major Task Force reports and II studies on special subjects such as subsidies and retirement. In total, these reports substantiate three-year ongoing savings of $424.4 billion, plus cash accelerations of $66 billion.

These are all analyzed and supported in great detail. Capsuled in terms of the functional problems to which they relate, the savings are as follows:

PPSS Savings Recommendations

	$ Billions	*% of Total*
Program Waste	$160.9	37.9%
System Failures	151.3	35.7
Personnel Mismanagement	90.9	21.4
Structural Deficiencies	12.7	3.0
Other Opportunities	8.6	2.0
Total	$424.4	100.0%

These data confirm our findings that system failures and personnel mismanagement together comprise well over one-half 57.1 percent, of the total savings possibilities. They are at the foundation of inefficiencies in the Federal Government. Program waste, which accounts for 37.9 percent of the savings recommendations, would also be substantially eliminated if proper systems and personnel management were in place.

The above underscores one of our most important recommendations, which is the establishment of an Office of Federal Management in the Executive Office of the President. This Federal Government top management office would include 0MB, GSA and OPM and have Government-wide responsibility for establishing, modernizing, and monitoring management systems.

If it is set up and staffed properly, it could go a long way to avoid in the future the thousands of deficiencies and examples of waste that we have identified. We would not feel our task complete if we just identified past deficiencies without recommendations for a management and organizational structure that would be best suited for preventing the errors of the past.

Additionally, the establishment of this new office would be beneficial in the implementation process of the PPSS recommendations.

In this regard, we believe that your Cabinet Council on Management and Administration, working in concert with the Office of Cabinet Affairs, is uniquely suited to lead a Government-wide effort to restore sound principles of management and efficiency to the Federal Government. While the Cabinet Council already has taken a leadership role in this regard, we urge you to call upon it to make implementation of the PPSS recommendations Government-wide its highest priority.

Mr. President, it was a great honor to have been asked by you to engage in this effort to identify ways to eliminate inefficiency, waste and abuse in the Federal Government. The project was structured and staffed to effect enduring improvement so that our children and grandchildren would not inherit a situation that would be devastating to them and to the values of our economic and social system. It was in this vein that we were able to enlist the 161 top executives from private business and other organizations to chair and to staff our 36 Task Forces at a cost to the private sector of over $75 million and at no cost to the Government.

All the participants join with me in thanking you for the opportunity to be of service and in looking forward to whatever additional help we may be able to provide to assure that the greatest practical results are obtained from the work of this Commission.

Respectfully,

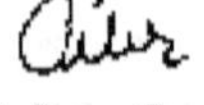

J. Peter Grace
Chairman

Bibliography

Andrew Collins, *From the Ashes of Angels - The Forbidden Legacy of a Fallen Race,* Bear & Company. (1996)

Bellamy, Edward, *Looking Backward* , Signet Classics, May 2000

Campbell Black, Henry, *Blacks Law Dictionary Abridged Sixth Edition*, West Publishing Co., St. Paul Min., 1991

Cooper, Peter, *Ideas For A Science Of Good Government: In Addresses, Letters And Articles On A Strictly National Currency, Tariff And Civil Service* , Trow's Printing and Bookbinding Co., New York, 1883

Dall, B. Curis, *My Exploited Father in Law*, Legion for the Survival of Freedom, Incorpora (January 1983)

Downes, John, Goodman Elliot, Jordan, *Dictionary of Finance and Investment terms*, Barron's Educational Series; 5th edition (September 1998):

Garner A., Bryan (Editor), *Blacks law dictionary, Eighth Edition* Thomson West (2004)

Golin, Jonathan, *The Bank Credit Analysis Handbook: A Guide for Analysts, Bankers and Investors*, John Wiley & Sons (August 10, 2001)

Mackey, A.G., *THE ENCYCLOPAEDIA [ENCYCLOPEDIA] OF FREEMASONRY AND ITS KINDRED SCIENCES* Moss & Co. 1873 and 1878

Money Facts: *169 Questions and Answers on Money- a Supplement to A Primer on Money, with Index, Subcommittee on Domestic Finance.* United States Congress. House. Banking and Currency Committee, Published 1964

Morris S. Brent, *Complete idiots guide to Freemasonry*, Penguin Group USA, New York, May 2006

Paulino, Jose M., *The Conspiracy Theory Fraud*. FactsMovement, New Jersey, October 2008

Paulino, Jose M., *The War on Terror Fraud*, FactsMovement, New Jersey, December 2008

Ramsey, Dave, *The Total Money Makeover: A proven plan for financial fitness*. Thomas Nelson Publishing., 2003

Task Force Members, *Building a North American Community*, Council on Foreign Relations Press, May 2005

'The FED today', a publication released
by the united states federal reserve education website designed to educate people on the history and purpose of the united states federal reserve system.

INDEX

A

B

E

F

M

N

V

W

THE SYMBOL OF THE SACRED MOVEMENT

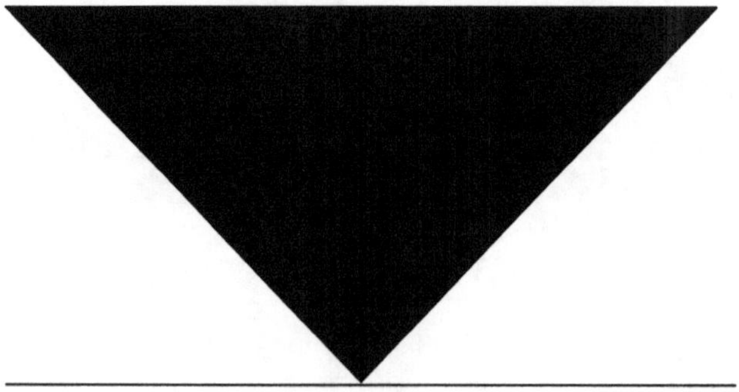

www.ingramcontent.com/pod-product-compliance
Lightning Source LLC
Chambersburg PA
CBHW071712170526
45165CB00005B/1984
* 9 7 8 1 4 4 0 4 6 3 4 7 1 *